The Alte Pinakothek   Munich

The Rubens Room in the Alte Pinakothek by J. Maass.

Erich Steingräber   Director General of the Bavarian State Paintings Collections

The Alte Pinakothek
Munich

© 1985 Scala Books

First published in 1985 by
Scala Books
143-149 Great Portland Street
London WIN 5FB

Reprinted 1998

Translated from the German by Elsie Callander
Photography: Artothek, Munich
Design: Alan Bartram

Printed and bound by
Società Editoriale L.
Trieste, Italy

ISBN 0 85667 220 3 (UK)
ISBN 0.935748.64.4 (USA)
Library of Congress No. 84-052513

The introductory text for the chapter on Old Netherlandish Painting
was written by Peter Eikemeier, and that on Flemish Painting by
Konrad Renger. The other introductory texts are based on the
following Alte Pinakothek publications:
Alte Pinakothek Catalogue II: Old German Painting compiled by Christian
Altgraf Salm and Gisela Goldberg (Munich, 1963).
Alte Pinakothek Catalogue III: Dutch Painting, compiled by Ernst
Brochhagen and Brigitte Knüttel (Munich, 1967).
Alte Pinakothek Catalogue IV: French and Spanish Painting, compiled by
Halldor Soehner and Johann Georg Prince of Hohenzollern, (Munich,
1972).
*From Giotto to Picasso: Masterpieces from the Bavarian State Paintings
Collections*, edited by Erich Steingräber (Munich, 1972).
Alte Pinakothek Catalogue V: Italian Painting, compiled by Rolf Kultzen
(Munich, 1975).

Front Cover
Self portrait by Albrecht Dürer

Back Cover
The seven joys of Mary by Hans Memling (detail)

Contents

Introduction

The Alte Pinakothek, which reflects the genealogy of the Wittelsbach rulers and their love of art, is one of the largest and finest paintings galleries in the world. This is true both of the pictures themselves and also of the museum buildings, which are the product of the congenial collaboration between King Ludwig I and his architect Leo von Klenze.

The first reference to ducal collecting is recorded in Johann Fickler's inventory of 1598 where he simply lists 3,407 miscellaneous objects of which, however, 778 are paintings. The most important items are two series of historical paintings which Duke Wilhelm IV (reigned 1508-1550) and his duchess Jacobea von Baden commissioned from the best known South German painters between 1528 and 1540 to adorn the walls of their Munich Residenz. These pictures celebrate manly virtue and bravery and extol the deeds of famous women, very much in accordance with the humanistic outlook of their patrons. Fifteen of them have been preserved, including *Alexander's battle* by Albrecht Altdorfer (p.123). This series, which was assembled in one room of the Alte Pinakothek in 1963, forms the nucleus of the Wittelsbach collection.

Maximilian I, who reigned 1597-1651, as Elector from 1623, was the most important German prince of his time and the first passionate collector of European stature among the Wittelsbachs. His favourite was Albrecht Dürer and he acquired eleven of his works, mostly in keen competition with the other great Dürer collector of the time, the Emperor Rudolf II. His efforts were crowned by the purchase of the *Four Apostles* (p.115) which Dürer had presented to his native town of Nuremberg. This period of the early seventeenth century, in which the greatest German painter came back into favour, is even referred to as the 'Dürer Renaissance'. At the same time Maximilian was also interested in Rubens, his contemporary.

In the person of Elector Max Emanuel (reigned 1679-1726), the paintings collection gained another outstanding collector. As governor of the Netherlands and also later as an emigré in France, he was particularly concerned with Flemish baroque painting and at the same time keenly interested in Italian, Dutch and French works. The most outstanding acquisition he made for the collection was his purchase in 1698 of 105 pictures from the Antwerp dealer Gisbert van Colen for the considerable sum of 90,000 Brabantine guilders. Among them were twelve paintings by Rubens including major works such as *The honeysuckle bower* (p.77), portraits of Hélène Fourment and the *Drunken Silenus* (p.79).

No substantial gains accrued to the collection under his successors Carl Albrecht (reigned 1726-1745) and Max III Joseph (reigned 1745-1777). With the second of these the Bavarian electoral line of the Wittelsbachs died out and was followed by the Palatine lines, to which the Bavarian royal house can be traced back. Among the Palatine Wittelsbachs, Elector Johann Wilhelm von der Pfalz (Jan Willem, who reigned 1690-1716 and had his seat in Düsseldorf) most resembled Max Emanuel in his talent as a collector, although he was more cautious and economical in his purchases. He, too, was particularly interested in Rubens, purchasing the *Battle of the amazons* (p.79) and others. His second wife, Maria Luisa, daughter of the Grand Duke Cosimo III of Tuscany, brought Raphael's *Holy Family from the Canigiani house* (p.16) and the *Holy Family* by Andrea del Sarto to Düsseldorf as part of her dowry. Johann Wilhelm particularly admired Luca Giordano and Adriaen van der Werff, whom he appointed as his court painter. Carl Theodor of the Palatine, who died without issue in 1799, was succeeded by Max IV Joseph of the Pfalz-Zweibrücken Wittelsbach line, who later became the first King of Bavaria (reigned 1799-1825). He had the galleries which he had inherited transferred from Düsseldorf and Mannheim to Munich, where they were merged with the Electoral gallery. His own still very young gallery in Carlsberg Castle, near Homburg on the Saar, was rescued from the approaching French army in 1793 and arrived intact in Munich in 1799. It contained mainly works by Dutch, Flemish and French artists, including Claude Lorrain's two paintings depicting the story of Hagar and Boucher's *Girl resting* (p.104).

The reputation of the Alte Pinakothek rests ultimately on the wealth of outstandingly fine works which were brought together when the various Wittelsbach galleries were merged in Munich. Wittelsbach domestic politics were not, however, the only factors contributing to the enlargement of the paintings collection; political events in the wake of the French Revolution also influenced it. In the course of the year 1803, when the church estates were taken over by the secular authorities in Bavaria, and when the old imperial cities were annexed along with the Franconian counties and foundations, about 1,500 paintings became the property of the State. These included significant Old German works such as the *Kaisheim Altar* by Hans Holbein the Elder and Michael Pacher's *Church Fathers' Altar* from the Neustift monastery in the Tyrol, which belonged to Bavaria from 1809 to 1815. Also among them was Giovanni Battista Tiepolo's *Adoration of the Kings* (p.30) from Munsterschwarzach. Prominent in all these rescue operations, which preserved many valuable works of art from being destroyed or thrown away, was Christian von Mannlich, the court painter from Zweibrücken, whom King Maximilian I had summoned to Munich and appointed as the director of the Bavarian galleries.

King Ludwig I (reigned 1825-1848), who was committed to the new spirit of classicism and romanticism, was the last Wittelsbach collector of real significance. His most spectacular achievement was the acquisition in 1827 of the famous collection of the Boisserée brothers, for which he paid, after lengthy negotiations, the large sum of 240,000 guilders. The collection contained 216 valuable Old Netherlandish and Old German paintings, particularly from Cologne, among them the *Three Kings Altar* of Rogier van der Weyden (p.38) and the *Saint Veronica with the Sudarium* (p.111), a gem of Cologne painting. Only a year later came the addition of the Prince of Oettingen-Wallerstein's collection—219 pictures at a cost of 80,000 guilders. These included valuable Old German paintings of the Dürer period, among them Dürer's *Portrait of Oswald Krel* and Altdorfer's *Danube landscape* (p.122). Among other purchases of Old German masters, special mention must be made of Dürer's self portrait. The Italian paintings were purchased almost exclusively by King Ludwig, many journeys and negotiations being necessary to secure masterpieces such as Perugino's *Vision of St Bernard* (p.14), Ghirlandaio's High Altar from Santa Maria Novella in Florence (p.15), *The Annunciation* by

Filippo Lippi (p.12) and Raphael's *Tempi Madonna* (p.17). In these transactions he was given expert advice by his gallery director Johann Georg von Dillis.

The bringing together of the various Wittelsbach galleries in Munich, along with King Ludwig I's numerous new acquisitions, soon called for a new building, and on 7 April 1826—Raphael's birthday—on the meadowland not far from the already existing Glyptothek in the Max-suburb, the king laid the foundation stone of the Pinakothek. The building—only later called the Ältere or Alte Pinakothek to distinguish it from the Neue Pinakothek—was no doubt called after the Pinakothek (*pinakes* = painting, *théké* = storage place) in the left wing of the propylaeum on the Acropolis in Athens, in which the consecrated paintings offered to Athena were kept. Within ten years Leo von Klenze had erected one of the earliest and finest gallery buildings in Europe and also one of the most technically advanced in terms of view of museum engineering.

Unfortunately, the splendid opportunities which the Munich art market offered in the second half of the nineteenth century were almost totally wasted. It was only towards the end of the century that a few significant purchases were made, namely Leonardo's *Virgin and child* (p.11), Antonella da Messina's portrait of the Virgin (p.18) and the portrait of Willem Croes by Frans Hals (p.53). During the short period in office of Hugo von Tschudi (he was appointed in 1909) some noticeable gaps were filled with works of masters which either had been beyond the range of the princely baroque collectors or had not corresponded to the taste of the romantic period: El Greco's *Disrobing of Christ* (p.88), Goya's *Plucked turkey* and Francesco Guardi's *Venetian gala concert* (p.34).

Although the Alte Pinakothek was badly damaged in the second world war, the paintings, which had been evacuated to various depositories, suffered no real harm. The gallery was re-built under Döllgast and re-opened in 1957.

Thanks to the museum's careful purchasing policy in the difficult post-war years, directors Ernst Buchner (1933-1945, 1953-1957), Eberhard Hanfstaengel (1945-1953), Kurt Martin (1957-1964) and Halldor Soehner (who, sadly, died after only four years in office, 1964-1968), the Alte Pinakothek was able to make a series of significant acquisitions. It was Soehner's great merit to secure for the musuem the patronage of the Bavarian Hypotheken und Wechsel Bank, with whose help it was possible to introduce works of the eighteenth century, hitherto hardly represented in the gallery. This opened up another new dimension in the Alte Pinakothek, and in 1967 the Francesco Guardi collection was opened to the public. In 1972 a special ceremony marked the presentation of three masterpieces so significant as to necessitate the reorganisation of the French room. These were the most beautiful portrait of Madame de Pompadour by François Boucher (p.105), the portrait of the Marquise de Baglion by Jean-Marc Nattier (p.102) and the portrait of the Marquise de Sorcy de Thelusson by Jacques-Louis David. This latter has been in the Neue Pinakothek since 1981. The Bavarian Landesbank has made available on loan two important early works of Boucher, and in 1967 special funds were provided by the State to purchase the portrait of Willem van Heythuysen by Frans Hals (p.53). After a rearrangement of the Dutch paintings, this painting has become the focus of that section.

Italian Painting

It is the excellence of the paintings in the Italian collection of the Alte Pinakothek, rather than their great number, that gives it its special distinction. This becomes particularly evident when one considers the prestigious stocks of Italian panel paintings of the fourteenth and fifteenth centuries which have come down to us as a result of Ludwig I's passion for collecting. Apart from the king's own artistic sensitivity, it was above all romantic ideas emanating from the religious and historical artistic sources, coupled with the striving for a renewal of the Christian faith that guided him in his selection of these particular pictures. Just how extensive his transactions eventually became can be truly discerned only when one considers how few examples of this type of picture had been handed down from the Wittelsbach heritage — in fact only Raphael's *Holy Family from the Canigiani house* (p.16) from Düsseldorf, Marco Basaiti's *Madonna with saints*, recorded in Schleissheim since 1748, and Jacopo de' Barbari's still life, which actually came into the Alte Pinakothek only in 1909. It is true that Ludwig was supported in his manifold endeavours by experienced advisers such as Johann Georg von Dillis (1749-1841) and Martin von Wagner (1777-1858), but the essential qualities for the success of the whole enterprise were ultimately provided by the never-flagging initiative and the astonishingly catholic taste of the king himself. The basic character of the collection of early Italian panel paintings built up at that time has not been radically changed even by later acquisitions. This has held good even in the face of such important additions as the Leonardo *Virgin and child* (p.11), purchased in 1899 from the Wetzlar dispensary in Günzburg, or the *Lamentation* by Liberale da Verona, acquired from Florentine dealers in 1890. Even Luca Signorelli's tondo of the Madonna, also acquired in Florence in 1894, and the *Virgin of the Annunciation* by Antonella da Messina (p.18) only serve to underline the coherence of this collection of exquisite works of art.

A true impression of the size of the collection can only be gained, however, when one takes account of a number of paintings which have had to be relegated to the store-room for various reasons. This is mainly because of the lack of space caused by today's more spacious style of hanging, but another contributory factor has been the attempt to incorporate into the collection works of art from periods which had long been denied the attention they deserved. These include Raffellino del Garbo's *Lamentation*, the picture of the Archangel with the young Tobias ascribed to Botticini, the four altar wings with saints by Granacci and the *Virgin and Child* formely claimed to be by Cesare da Sesto but today correctly attributed to Alonso Berruguete.

On the other hand, the stocks of Venetian paintings of the sixteenth century, which have been in the Alte Pinakothek since its inception, have retained their original prominence. Among them are such important masterpieces as *Christ with the crown of thorns* by Titian (p.22) and Tintoretto's extensive 'Gonzaga' cycle (p.25).

Ultimately, Ludwig's special predilections worked to the detriment of the seventeenth and eighteenth-century Italian schools as regards the amount of space they were allotted in the Alte Pinakothek. Because of the somewhat invidious position Baroque painting had fallen into in his time, vis-à-vis the classicism of the High Renaissance, only a relatively limited number of examples found their way into the Alte Pinakothek. The gallery's display scheme had already been designed, even down to structural details, making further additions difficult. At all events, the selection made at that time is completely disproportionate to the number of paintings of this period which were actually available, having found their way first into the Munich Hofgarten gallery around the turn of the nineteenth century, principally from Schleissheim, Düsseldorf and Mannheim. Eventually it was possible to clear only one of the main rooms of the Alte Pinakothek to accommodate them, along with a series of side galleries. In 1970 the Italian room was enriched by the acquisition of two landscapes by Annibale Carracci.

The eighteenth century, which by its very nature was the most immediately exposed to the adverse criticism of classicism, was almost completely passed over at the time the Alte Pinakothek was being furnished. The only exceptions were Giovanni Battista Tiepolo's *Adoration of the Kings* (p.30), painted between 1751 and 1753 for the monastery of Schwarzach in Franconia and transferred to Munich as early as 1804 in the course of the secularisation taking place at that time, and a series of vedute, originally comprising four paintings, by Antonio Canaletto. The systematic planning of additions in this area began only in our own century and as on so many other occasions, the initiative was taken by Hugo von Tschudi when he purchased Francesco Guardi's *Venetian gala concert* (p.34) in 1909. Enduring interest in this artist was stimulated by the patronage of the Bavarian Hypotheken und Wechsel Bank, which meant that the Bank's collection of eighteenth-century masterpieces already on loan to the gallery could be enlarged by the purchase of additional paintings by Guardi, along with works by Pietro Longhi, Giovanni Battista Battoni, Rosalba Carriera, Alessandro Magnasco and Michele Marieschi.

This impressive group was agreeably rounded off by Francesco Guardi's view of Santa Maria della Salute, which was placed at the disposal of the gallery by the Association for the Promotion of the Alte Pinakothek. Already in 1925 Giovanni Battista Pittoni's *Birth of Christ*, which had come from the Castle of Bayreuth, had found its way into the Alte Pinakothek; in 1939 the original sketch for Pittoni's depiction of Eustachius, painted around 1730, was added, purchased by the Friends of the Gallery. Finally, the inclusion of a notable work by Giovanni Battista Piazetta to fill a particularly glaring gap has made the collection of eighteenth-century Italian paintings still more representative.

MARY MAGDALENE WITH THE BOX OF
OINTMENT
**Segna di Buonaventura (working in
Siena between 1298 and 1327),** *c* 1310
Poplar, gold ground; frame 19th century;
44 x 59cm
The most 'ancient' picture in the Alte
Pinakothek, because still strongly indebted
to Byzantine models.
Purchased from Munich art dealers in
1921. (9038)

THE ASCENSION OF THE VIRGIN
Sienese Master (working *c* 1340**),** *c* 1340
Poplar, gold ground; 72.5 x 32.5cm
In the upper part, the Coronation of the
Virgin is represented on a smaller scale. The
finely stamped gilded background lends the
hieratic composition an aura which is
independent of space and time.
Purchased by Crown Prince Ludwig in
1825. (WAF 671)

THE LAST SUPPER
Giotto di Bondone (b. Colle di
Vespignagno, near Florence, 1266,
d. Florence 1337), probably soon after
1306
Chestnut; 42.5 x 43.2cm
The sober composition, dispensing with all
ornamental details, in which the plastically
rounded figures are arranged parallel to
the picture in a narrow box-room, reveals
Giotto as a fresco painter accustomed to
the monumental format. The picture is one
of a series of seven panels, two others of
which are preserved in the Alte Pinakothek.
Sent as a present to Crown Prince Ludwig
in 1805: the two other panels were
purchased from Count Lucchesi by King
Maximilian I in 1813. (643)

THE DEATH OF THE NOBLEMAN OF CELANO
Taddeo Gaddi (b. Florence *c* 1300
d. Florence 1366), *c* 1340
Poplar, gold ground; in original quatrefoil
frame; 34.8 x 30.7cm
The companion panel, *St Francis Offering
the Sultan Ordeal by Fire,* is also in the
Alte Pinakothek. Together with twenty-four
other pictures (twenty-two in Florence,
Galleria dell' Accademia; two in Berlin,
Staatliche Museen), they originally formed
the panels of the doors of a sacristy
cupboard in Santa Croce in Florence. The
inner panels showed scenes from the life
of Christ, the outer ones pictures from the
life of St Francis (according to Bonaventura's
Vita).
Acquired 1940. (10676)

VIRGIN AND CHILD
Masolino (Tommaso di Cristoforo Fini:
b. Panicale di Valdarno *c* 1383,
d. before 1447), *c* 1435/40
Chestnut, gold ground; 95.5 x 57cm
Antique type of 'Madonna dell'Umiltà', the
humble mother of God. The very
pronounced corporeality of the figures,
particularly of the child, reveals the influence
of Masaccio, although the picture in
general is still beholden to the international
'Soft Style'.
Acquired by King Ludwig I later than 1826.
(WAF 264)

▽
SAINTS COSMAS AND DAMIAN WITH THEIR
BROTHERS BEFORE THE PROCONSUL LYSIAS
Fra Angelico (Fra Giovanni da Fiesole:
b. Vicchio, near Florence, 1386/1400,
d. Rome 1455), before 1440
Poplar; 37.8 x 46.6cm
Cosmas and Damian, patrons of the city of
Florence and of the Medici, were Christian
twin brothers who practised the art of
healing without charging fees and in this
way won over many souls to Christianity.
The graceful narrative tone combines
late medieval colourfulness and 'naivety'
with the clarity of the early Renaissance in
the compositional structure. There are a
further three companion panels in the Alte
Pinakothek, and five more in Paris,
Washington and Dublin. From the predella
of the high altar of the monastery church
of San Marco in Florence, erected in 1440.
Acquired by Crown Prince Ludwig in 1822.
(WAF 36)

VIRGIN AND CHILD
Leonardo da Vinci (b. Villa Anchiana near Vinci (Empoli) 1452, d. Chateau de Cloux near Amboise 1519), *c* 1473
Poplar; 62 x 47.5cm

The famous *sfumato* of Leonardo has triumphed over the bright local colour of Quattrocento painting. The composition is no longer the sum of its individual parts but the reflection of a new, total world-view. Purchased from Dr A. Haug in Günzburg in 1899, after Adolph Bayersdorfer had recognized the hand of Leonardo in a previously unknown work. (7779)

THE ANNUNCIATION
Fra Filippo Lippi (b. Florence *c* 1406, d. Spoleto 1469), *c* 1450
Poplar; 203 x 186cm
The scene, framed by early Renaissance architecture in delicate colours, is reminiscent of the medieval *Hortus conclusus* as an allusion to the immaculate purity of the mother of God.
The altar picture, which comes from the monastery church of the Suore Murate (an enclosed order of nuns) in Florence, was purchased for the royal collection in Munich at the beginning of the 19th century. (1072)

VIRGIN AND CHILD
Fra Filippo Lippi (b. Florence *c* 1406, d. Spoleto 1469), *c* 1465
Chestnut; 76.3 x 54.2cm
In his late works the painter has gone beyond the bright local colour of his early period. The forward-looking conception of landscape is particularly noteworthy. Purchased for Crown Prince Ludwig from the Abbate Rivanni in Florence in 1808. (647)

LAMENTATION
Sandro Botticelli (b. Florence c **1445,
d. Florence 1510), after 1490**
Poplar; 140 x 207cm
The austere, ascetic manner of expression
reflects the enduring impression made
on the painter by Savanarola's sermons on
repentance.
The picture comes from the Paolino
monastery in Florence and was acquired by
Crown Prince Ludwig in 1814. (1075)

VIRGIN AND CHILD
Luca Signorelli (b. Cortona c **1445/50,
d. Cortona 1523),** c **1495**
Lime wood; diam. 87cm
The tondo was particularly popular in the
Florentine renaissance. The motif of the
classical 'Boy with a Thorn' appearing in
the background was taken as a possible
allusion to the life of unredeemed man in
his natural state.
Acquired from the Ginori Palace in Florence
in 1894. (7931)

THE VISION OF ST BERNARD
Pietro Perugino (b. Città della Pieve
(Umbria) 1445, d. Fontignano
(Perugia) 1523), *c* 1490/94
Chestnut; 173 x 170cm

Legend has it that the mother of God,
accompanied by angels, appeared to St
Bernard of Clairvaux. Behind the saint are
John the Evangelist and the apostle
Bartholomew. This altarpiece, which can be
regarded as one of the painter's major
works, was executed for the chapel of the
Nasi family in Santa Maria Maddalena
dei Pazzi in Florence.
Purchased by King Ludwig I from the
Capponi house in Florence in 1829/30.
(WAF 764)

THE HIGH ALTAR OF SANTA MARIA NOVELLA
IN FLORENCE
**Domenico Ghirlandaio (b. Florence
1449, d. Florence 1494),** *c* **1494**
Poplar; 221 x 198cm (central panel)
The altar, donated by Giovanni Tornabuoni,
was not quite completed at the time of the
painter's death. The central panel,
composed on strictly architectonic lines,
shows Mary with the Child and Saints
Dominic, Michael, John the Baptist and
John the Evangelist, while the side panels
(also in the Alte Pinakothek) show St
Catherine of Siena and St Laurence.
After the altar was dismantled in 1804,
Crown Prince Ludwig purchased the panels
from the Medici house in Florence in
1816. Other parts of the altar are to be
found in the museum in Budapest and
amongst art dealers. (1078)

MADONNA IN THE ROSE BOWER
Francesco Francia (Francesco Raibolini:
b. Bologna *c* 1450, d. Bologna 1517),
signed, immediately after 1500
Poplar; 174.5 x 131.5cm
From the late Middle Ages onwards, the rose
bower was regularly used to symbolize the
virtues of the Virgin, using the language
of flowers. This devotional picture, painted
for the Capuchin church in Modena,
found its way by devious paths into the
collection of the Empress Josephine in
Malmaison, from which it was purchased
by Crown Prince Ludwig in 1815. (994)

▽

HOLY FAMILY WITH THE YOUNG ST JOHN
Lorenzo di Credi (b. Florence 1459,
d. Florence 1537), *c* 1510
Poplar; diam. 98.5cm
Akin to the early works of Fra Bartolomeo.
The painting was for many years taken
to be the product of several hands but the
high painterly qualities today confirm the
attribution to one painter.
Purchased in Florence for Crown Prince
Ludwig in 1815. (WAF 191)

16

▷
THE TEMPI MADONNA
**Raphael (Raffaello Santi: b. Urbino
1483, d. Rome 1520),** *c* 1507
Chestnut; 75 x 51cm
This picture—one of the major works of the
Florentine period—came from the Tempi
house in Florence and was finally purchased
by King Ludwig I in 1809 after many
years of effort. (WAF 796)

◁
THE HOLY FAMILY FROM THE CANIGIANI
HOUSE
**Raphael (Raffaello Santi: b. Urbino
1483, d. Rome 1520),** *c* 1505/06
Lime wood; 131 x 107cm
This picture, painted by Raphael for
Domenico Canigiani at the beginning of his
Florentine period, invites comparison,
above all in the presentation of the figures,
with Fra Bartolomeo and Leonardo. The
putti, painted over in the late 18th century,
were restored in 1983.
The painting found its way into the
Düsseldorf gallery as a gift from Archduke
Cosimo III of Tuscany to his son-in-law,
Elector Johann Wilhelm of the Palatine.
(476)

▷
MADONNA DELLA TENDA (WITH THE
CURTAIN)
**Raphael (Raffaello Santi: b. Urbino
1483, d. Rome 1520),** *c* 1513/14
Chestnut; 65.8 x 51.2cm
The mature style of the figures, which
almost fill the area of the picture, invites
comparison with Michelangelo's Sistine
Chapel ceiling.
The picture, which is recorded as being
in the Escorial from the 17th century until
1809, found its way to England during
the Napoleonic wars and it was there
acquired by Crown Prince Ludwig in 1819.
(WAF 797)

VIRGIN OF THE ANNUNCIATION
Antonella da Messina (b. Messina
c **1430, d. Messina 1479),** *c* **1473/74**
Walnut; 42.5 x 32.8cm
Probably from a diptych, the other half of
which would show the angel of the
annunciation. The Old Netherlandish
models are unmistakable.
Purchased from art dealers in Munich in
1897. (8054)

▽

HOLY FAMILY WITH THE YOUNG ST JOHN
Domenico Beccafumi (real name
Mecuccio or Mecarino: b. near Siena
1486, d. Siena 1551), *c* **1515**
Chestnut; diam. 113cm
Acquired by Crown Prince Ludwig in Siena
in 1816. (1073)

THE MYSTICAL MARRIAGE OF ST CATHERINE
Lorenzo Lotto (b. Venice *c* **1480,**
d. Loreto 1556), signed, between 1505
and 1508
Panel; 71.3 x 91.2cm
After Catherine, daughter of King Costus
of Cyprus, had been converted to
Christianity by baptism, the mother of God
appeared to her in a dream with the Christ
child, who married her.
Transferred from the Prince Bishop's
residence in Würzburg to Munich in
1804. (32)

VIRGIN AND CHILD WITH SAINTS MARY
MAGDALENE AND JEROME
**Giovanni Battista Cima da Conegliano
(b. Conegliano (Treviso) 1459,
d. Conegliano c 1517/18), signed,
c 1496**
Lime wood; 79.6 x 122.9cm

A *sacra conversazione*, of the type that
Antonello da Messina had created in his
San Cassiano altarpiece in Venice in 1475.
From the Manin collection in Venice.
Purchased for Crown Prince Ludwig in Paris
in 1815 from the estate of the Empress
Josephine. (992)

STILL LIFE WITH PARTRIDGE, GLOVES AND
CROSS-BOW ARROW
**Jacapo de' Barbari (b. Venice c 1440,
d. in the Netherlands before 1515),
signed and dated 1504**
Lime wood; 52 x 42.5cm
According to the inventories of art objects
which have come down to us, we are
dealing here — if this was in fact painted as
a picture in its own right — with the
oldest extant still life in European panel
painting. A short time later Dürer and
Cranach the Elder painted still life
aquarelles.
Recorded as being in Neuburg Castle on
the Danube from 1764 onwards.
Transferred to Schleissheim Castle in 1804.
(5066)

VIRGIN AND CHILD IN EVENING LANDSCAPE
Titian (Tiziano Vecellio: b. Pieve di Cadore *c* **1487/90, d. Venice 1576), signed (later?),** *c* **1560**
Canvas; 173.5 x 132.7 cm
Titian's late style reveals itself in the richly-graded palette of substantially applied colours.
Probably in the possession of Philip II of Spain, recorded as being in the Escorial in 1606. Taken from there by Joseph Bonaparte in 1809 and given by him to General Sebastiani, from whom it was purchased for King Maximilian I by J.G. Dillis in 1814. (464)

▷
EMPEROR KARL V
Titian (Tiziano Vecellio; b. Pieve di Cadore *c* **1487/90, d. Venice 1576), signed and dated 1548**
Canvas; 203.5 x 122cm
Commissioned by the Emperor and executed during Titian's stay in Augsburg in 1548. Whereas the Madrid portrait completed at the same time represents the Emperor in armour as the victor of the Battle of Mühldorf, this portrait brings out the human features of the ageing ruler afflicted by gout. From the Elector's gallery in Munich. (632)

PORTRAIT OF A YOUNG MAN
Titian (Tiziano Vecellio; b. Pieve di Cadore *c* **1487/90, d. Venice 1576),** *c* **1520**
Canvas mounted on oak; 89.3 x 74.3cm
The Arcadian spirit of the court of the muses in Asolo, to which Giorgione also belonged (Giorgione being an influential model for the young Titian) comes through clearly in the somewhat dreamy, hitherto unknown conception of portraiture which particularly delineates generosity and spirituality.
From the Düsseldorf gallery. (517)

VIRGIN AND CHILD WITH ST ANTHONY
AND THE YOUNG ST JOHN
**Giovanni Cariani (Giovanni de' Busi:
probably b. Venice *c* 1480, d. 1547),
c 1540**
Canvas; 164 x 199.5cm
Formerly attributed to Titian. The striking
thing is the landscape—composed like a
stage set, and obviously using ideas from
Netherlandish painters working in the
Veneto.
Purchased from art dealers in Munich in
1923. (9210)

PORTRAIT OF A CLERIC
**Moretto da Brescia (Alessandro
Bonvicino: b. Brescia *c* 1498,
d. Brescia 1554), *c* 1550**
Canvas; 101.5 x 78cm
Lombardian traditions and Venetian
influence merge here in the portraiture art
of the Brescian school of painters of the
High Renaissance.
Purchased in 1838 from the estate of the
Marchese Canova, Venice. (WAF 683)

◁
CHRIST WITH THE CROWN OF THORNS
**Titian (Tiziano Vecellio: b. Pieve di
Cadore *c* 1487/90, d. Venice 1576),
late work**
Canvas; 280 x 182cm
Developed entirely from the use of colour—
there is virtually no drawing—this picture
can be regarded as the epitome of Titian's rich
life's work. Along with Dürer's *Four Apostles*,
which also constitutes a human as well
as an artistic testament, it is surely one of the
most unforgettable masterpieces in the
Alte Pinakothek.
First mentioned in the Schleissheim
inventory in 1748. (2272)

CHRIST AT THE HOUSE OF MARY
AND MARTHA
**Tintoretto (Jacopo Robusti: b. Venice
1518, d. Venice 1594), signed** *c* **1580**
Canvas; 200 x 132cm
Luke 10:38-42. Stylistically related to
the paintings in the Scuola di San Rocco.
Probably donated by the Welser family
as an altarpiece for the church of the
Dominicans in Augsburg.
Transferred from there to Munich in 1803
when the church possessions were dispersed.
(4788)

PORTRAIT OF A LADY
**Veronese (Paolo Caliari: b. Verona
1528, d. Venice 1588), soon after 1570**
Canvas; 117.3 x 100.8cm
Although unknown, the subject embodies
very strikingly the rich, confident partrician
class of Venice.
Known to have been in the Schleissheim
gallery from 1748. (594)

▷
LODOVICO II GONZAGA DEFEATING THE
VENETIANS ON THE ETSCH AT
LEGNANO, 1439
**Tintoretto (Jacopo Robusti: b. Venice
1518, d. Venice 1594), completed 1579**
Canvas; 273 x 385.5cm
From the series of eight historical paintings
which Duke Guglielmo commissioned for
the Palazzo Ducale in Mantua. Stylistically
they are akin to the contemporary paintings
in the Scuola di San Rocco in Venice.
Probably acquired by Elector Max Emanuel;
recorded as being in Schleissheim from
1748 onwards. (7304)

VENUS AND MARS SURPRISED BY VULCAN
Tintoretto (Jacopo Robusti: b. Venice
1518, d. Venice 1594), *c* 1555
Canvas; 135 x 198cm
The adulterers Venus and Mars are found
guilty and subsequently suffer the

derision of the Gods (8th Song of the
Odyssey).
Probably from Count Arundel's collection,
from which it found its way into the
possession of the Duke of Devonshire.
Purchased from F.A. Kaulbach, Munich, in
1925. (9257)

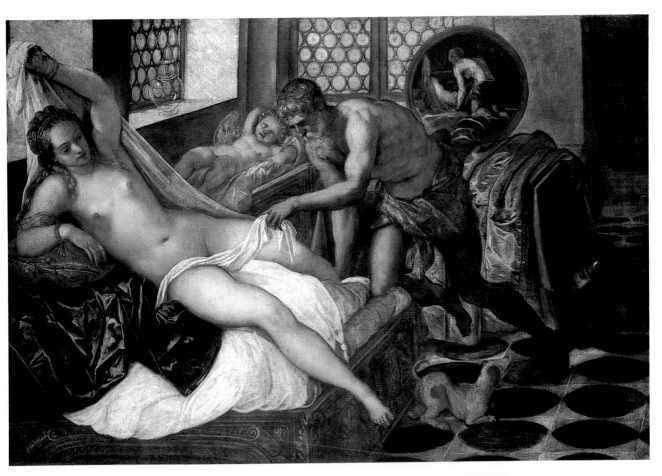

MARTHA UPBRAIDS HER SISTER MARY
Orazio Gentileschi (b. Pisa 1577, d. Rome 1653), *c* 1620
Canvas; 133 x 155cm
The interpretation of this picture, composed sympathetically and with powerful plasticity to illustrate Luke 10:38-42, is still in doubt. At all events, it is probably intended to convey the admonishing of Vanity (with the mirror) by Virtue (in simple, loose clothing).
The gift of Georg and Otto Schäfer, Schweinfurt, for the re-opening of the Alte Pinakothek in 1957. (12726)

VIRGIN AND CHILD WITH ST BRUNO
Girolamo Bedoli-Mazzola (b. Viadana (Cremona) *c* 1500, **d. Parma 1569),** *c* 1533/35
Lime wood; 27.3 x 21.6cm
St Bruno was the founder of the Carthusian order. There are several versions of this markedly manneristic composition.
From Maximilian I's private gallery. (5289)

△
THE VISION OF ST FRANCIS
Carlo Saraceni (b. Venice *c* 1580/85, **d. Venice 1620), signed, late work**
Canvas; 242 x 165cm
The blind saint, marked out by death, is comforted by the sound of heavenly music. The Caravaggesque chiaroscuro is muted by the Venetian palette. Probably procured by Sebastian Füll, an agent of Elector Maximilian I, and brought to Munich in 1620. Recorded as being in the Castle of Schleissheim from 1740 onwards. (113)

▷
LANDSCAPE WITH WOMEN BATHING
Annibale Carracci (b. Bologna 1560, d. Rome 1609), *c* 1590
Canvas; 99 x 150.5 cm
This picture, along with another one important in the history of landscape painting and also in the Alte Pinakothek, was probably originally part of the interior decoration of a room.
Purchased from art dealers in London in 1979. (14617)

THE ASCENSION OF THE VIRGIN
Guido Reni (b. Calvenzano near Bologna 1575, d. Bologna 1642), 1631/42
Silk; 295 x 208cm
Formerly the high altar of the church of the Confraternity of Santa Maria degli Angioli di Spilamberto (Modena). A typical example of Bolognese baroque painting in classicistic mood, contrasting markedly with the *verismo* of the Caravaggists.
From the Düsseldorf gallery. (446)

A CYNICAL PHILOSOPHER
Luca Giordano (b. Naples 1634,
d. Naples 1705), *c* 1660
Canvas; 131 x 103cm
A companion piece is also in the Alte
Pinakothek. The realistic conception of
portrait painting is the result of coming to
grips with the Caravaggesque style of Ribera.
The Greek philosophical school of the
Cynics stood for a frugal life-style.
From the Düsseldorf gallery. (492)

LANDSCAPE WITH MONKS
Allessandro Magnasco (b. Genoa 1667,
d. Genoa 1749), *c* 1720/30
Canvas; 237.5 x 178.8cm
Magnasco's fanciful, visionary depiction
of landscape is Genoa's last major
contribution to Italian baroque painting.
Purchased from a private Venetian source
for the collection of the Bavarian
Hypotheken- und Wechsel-Bank in the
Alte Pinakothek. (HUW 25)

ERMINIA AMONG THE SHEPHERDS
Bernardo Cavallino (b. Naples 1615,
d. Naples 1656) *c* 1650/55
Canvas; diam. 50.2cm
Companion picture to *Erminia and the
Wounded Tancred*, also in the Alte Pinakothek.
From Tasso's *Gerusalemme Liberata* (VII: 6-7).
From the Mannheim gallery. (960)

◁

THE ADORATION OF THE KINGS
**Giovanni Battista Tiepolo (b. Venice
1695, d. Madrid 1770), signed and
dated 1753**
Canvas; 408 x 210.5cm
Altar picture for the monastery of
Schwarzach (Lower Franconia). This great
festive composition goes right back, via
Sebastiano Ricci, to Veronese.
Acquired from the monastery of Schwarzach
in 1804 when its possessions were
dispersed. (1159)

▷

POPE CLEMENS WORSHIPPING THE TRINITY
**Giovanni Battista Tiepolo (b. Venice
1696, d. Madrid 1770),** *c* **1739**
Canvas; 488 x 256cm
Commissioned by Elector Clemens August
of Cologne and executed for the Chorfrauen
church of Nymphenburg Castle (destroyed
in 1943). The donor is clearly identifying
himself with his saintly namesake in
this extremely 'theatrically' composed
altar picture.
Received on loan from the Chorfrauen
church of Nymphenburg Castle in 1938.
(877)

31

△
VIEW OF THE PIAZETTA DEI LEONI
**Michele Marieschi (b. Venice 1710,
d. Venice 1744),** *c* 1740
Canvas; 54.5 x 83.6cm
A companion piece, *The Grand Canal near
the Ca' Pesaro* is also in the Alte Pinakothek.
The strangely 'naïve' views of Venice by
Marieschi fall, art-historically, between
the vedute of Canaletto and Guardi.
Purchased from London art-dealers in
1983. (14788)

▷
REGATTA ON THE CANALE DELLA GIUDECCA
**Francesco Guardi (b. Venice 1712,
d. Venice 1793),** *c* 1784/89
Canvas; 61 x 93cm
Companion piece to the *Bacino di San
Marco* in the Emil Böhrle collection, Zürich.
It gives the impression of a photograph
taken with a wide-angled lens: the painter
was not primarily concerned with
topographical accuracy but rather with the
sparkling depiction of a romantically
grandiose panorama.

Purchased from London art dealers in
1975 for the collection of the Bavarian
Hypotheken- and Wechsel-Bank in the
Alte Pinakothek. (HUW 34)

PIAZETTA AND BACINO DI SAN MARCO IN
VENICE
**Canaletto (Antonio Canal b. Venice
1697, d. Venice 1768),** *c* **1730/40**
Canvas; 69.1 x 94.5cm
Companion piece to *Santa Maria della
Salute,* also in the Alte Pinakothek.
These vedute, characterized by cool, sober
observation, were purchased by King
Ludwig I from the estate of the sculptor
Antonio Canova along with two other
companion pictures (now in the H. J. Joel
collection, London).

THE GRAND CANAL NEAR SAN GEREMIA
**Francesco Guardi (b. Venice 1712,
d. Venice 1793),** *c* **1760**
Canvas; 71.5 x 120cm
A companion piece showing the Rialto
bridge is also in the Alte Pinakothek. The
meticulously detailed depiction of the locality
reveals the influence of Canaletto and the
use of the camera obscura.
Purchased from London art dealers in
1967 for the collection of the Bavarian
Hypotheken- and Wechsel-Bank in the Alte
Pinakothek. (HUW 8)

VENETIAN GALA CONCERT
Franceso Guardi (b. Venice 1712, d. Venice 1793), *c* **1782**
Canvas; 67.7 x 90.5cm
Part of a cycle of paintings, commissioned by the senate on the occasion of the visit of the Russian Grand Duke Paul Petrovitch and his wife Maria Feodorovna in 1782, and painted in Venice. The subject is the ladies' concert in the Scala dei Filarmonici under the auspices of the old procurators. Seldom in the history of painting have tones of colour and sound been so felicitously mingled.
Purchased from English art dealers (the Tschudi-Donation). (8574)

THE GAME OF CARDS
Pietro Longhi (b. Venice 1702, d. Venice 1785), *c* **1760**
Canvas; 62 x 49cm
As nearly always in Longhi's Venetian 'conversation pieces', the dividing lines between reality and the make-believe world of the theatre are fluid.
Purchased from London art dealers in 1971. (HUW 17)

Old Netherlandish Painting

The small but select collection of Old Netherlandish paintings in the Alte Pinakothek comprises works from the artistically fruitful period between the middle of the fifteenth century and the 1620s, mostly from Flanders and Brabant, the two northerly provinces of present-day Belgium whose influence was then predominant. Bruges and Ghent, Brussels, Liège and later Antwerp were centres of trade and commerce, in which the arts also flourished.

Some of these pictures had found their way to Germany at quite an early date as a result of the close trade relations, through the Hanseatic League, between the city of Cologne and the Netherlands, where works were commissioned and painted for Cologne churches. Deprived of their traditional home as a result of the secularisation of ecclesiastical estates at the beginning of the nineteenth century, they came into the possession of the brothers Melchior and Sulpiz Boisserée, dedicated Cologne collectors whose appreciation of art had been shaped by the enthusiasm of romantic poets and philosophers for the hitherto little esteemed 'primitive' art of the Middle Ages. This collection was purchased by King Ludwig I of Bavaria in 1827 and its rich stocks became a cornerstone of the Alte Pinakothek.

The oldest work in the Old Netherlandish section, and at the same time the outstanding focal point, is the *Three Kings Altar* (p.38) from St Columba's in Cologne, painted by the Brussels urban painter Rogier van der Weyden around 1455. Harmony of line and purity of colour are evidence of the heights of spiritual and artistic perfection achieved by this school in its finest moments.

The art of Dieric Bouts, on the other hand, is, as Max J. Friedländer observed, 'more concerned with the emotions'. This painter, working in Liège, was one of the first to include in his pictures the sentimental values of landscape and of the changing light at different times of day. This newly acquired element of expression is already clearly in evidence in the *Taking of Christ* (p.40) which was once the inside of the left wing of a triptych from the church of St Laurenz in Cologne. In the *Pearl of Brabant* (p.39), the small, exquisite household altar belonging to a Liège patrician family, it becomes the determining factor of the pictorial composition. The miniature-like delicacy of the painting, the soft, jewel-like brightness of the colour and the striking immediacy of the rendering combine in this work to give an enchanting effect, accentuated by the picture's impeccable state of preservation.

Hans Memling, a native of the Middle Rhine area who came to fame in Bruges, is also represented by a major work in the collection. The wide, panoramic landscape with the *Seven joys of Mary* (p.42/3), which provides scope for a large number of biblical and legendary episodes from the life of Christ and his mother, was formerly an altar panel in a small chapel in the Frauenkirche in Bruges. In the course of an eighteenth-century modernisation it was felt to be outmoded, was removed and came into the possession of the

Empress Josephine Beauharnais. Later, via art dealers, it came into the hands of the Boisserée brothers. Since then this gem of unspectacular, tenderly intimate narrative skill has been one of the pieces most admired by the public in the collection. The rather middle-class, decent character of Bruges art, which at the same time has a pleasing warmth of feeling, is again expressed in the romantic *Rest during the flight into Egypt* by Adriaen Isenbrant (p.45) who, through the influence of Gerard David, could be said to be a 'descendant' of Memling.

Although the paintings which had belonged to the Boisserée brothers form the nucleus of the Old Netherlandish stocks in Munich, there were already a few significant works from this area in the collection before their acquisition and other followed later. Elector Maximilian, although a passionate admirer of Dürer, had by no means confined his interest to the work of the Nüremberg master. His collector's enthusiasm was also directed towards Dürer's German and Netherlandish contemporaries who, like Dürer, had portrayed man in his newly won freedom and responsibility as an individual, having shaken off his cramping medieval fetters. Among the Old Netherlandish paintings housed in the private gallery in the Residenz in Munich was the panel with the figures of the Emperor Constantine and his mother St Helen (p.45) — presumably a fragment of a larger altar work. This panel by the Leyden painter Cornelis Engebrechtsz is remarkable both iconographically and in the expressive style of its figures. Lucas van Leyden, an important disciple of Engebrechtsz is represented with a diptych, *Virgin and Child with St Mary Magdalene and donor* (p.45). This work, reminiscent of Dürer and outstanding in its high artistic quality, had formerly been in Emperor Rudolf II's collection in Prague and then in the possession of Maximilian, his keenest rival in collecting. It is now not possible to reconstruct how it found its way to Munich although some kind of exchange of paintings seems likely. At all events, on its arrival there it was altered, like numerous other pictures in Maximilian's collection, by merging the two parts of the diptych into one and trimming the top to form a rectangular panel. (Parts of the addition were later removed.)

The *Danae* by Jan Gossaert (p.46) also came from the imperial collection in Prague, although it is only recorded as being in Munich from the middle of the eighteenth century. This highly artificial work aptly characterises the situation which the artists of the North found themselves facing in the first decades of the sixteenth century. With their roots in their native tradition, they were confronted by the new ideas of the Renaissance which were streaming in, ever more powerfully, from Italy. These ideas reveal themselves here not only in the themes but also in the feeling for bodies and space.

Hieronymus Bosch's infernal portrayal of the Last Judgment (p.44), of which only a relatively small fragment has survived from a panel which probably originally measured several square metres, comes from a world peopled by creatures completely unknown to human evolution. It is recorded as being in the collection since the early nineteenth century, originating from an unknown source.

ST LUKE DRAWING THE VIRGIN
**Rogier van der Weyden (b. Tournai
1399 or 1400, d. Brussels 1464),** *c* 1450
Oak; 138 x 110cm
Legend has it that St Luke the Evangelist,
patron saint of painters, made the authentic
portrait of the mother of God. This
composition (of which three other versions
exist from the 15th century, in Boston,
Leningrad and Bruges), goes back to the
Madonna of Chancellor Rolin (Paris, Louvre).
Most striking here are the two figures with
their backs to the viewer in the middle
ground, drawing the eyes to the river
landscape which is depicted in detail.
Purchased by King Ludwig I in 1827 as
part of the Boisserée collection. (WAF 1188)

THREE KINGS ALTAR (COLUMBA ALTAR)
Rogier van der Weyden (b. Tournai 1399 or 1400, d. Brussels 1464), *c* 1455
Oak; 138 x 153cm (central panel)
Central panel: *Adoration of the Kings.* Left wing: *Annunciation.* Right wing: *The Presentation in the Temple.* Since the reverse sides of the altar wings are not painted, the triptych was clearly not intended to be closed. Donated by the Bürgermeister (Mayor) of Cologne, Goedert von den Wasserfass to St Columba's in Cologne. After the Dissolution the altar, which must rank as one of the major works of Old Netherlandish painting, found its way into the Boisserée collection in Cologne, where Goethe admired it.
This collection was purchased by King Ludwig I in 1827. (WAF 1189)

'PEARL OF BRABANT' ALTARPIECE

Dieric Bouts (b. Haarlem between 1410 and 1420, d. Louvain 1475), *c* 1470

Altarpiece with side-wings

Oak; 62.6 x 62.6cm (central panel)

Central panel: *Adoration of the Kings.*
Left wing (inside): *John the Baptist,* (outside): *St Catherine.* Right wing (inside): *St Christopher,* (outside): *St Barbara.* The triptych, which once no doubt served private devotion, is conspicuous by its enamel-like colouring shining from the depths and by the exciting atmosphere. The name 'Pearl of Brabant' is known to have been used only since the beginning of this century.

Purchased by the Boisserée brothers from a private owner in Malines in 1813. Acquired by King Ludwig I with the Boisserée collection in 1827. (WAF 76)

THE TAKING OF CHRIST
**Dieric Bouts (b. Haarlem between 1410
and 1420, d. Louvain 1475),** *c* 1450/60
Part of an altarpiece with side-wings
Oak; 105 x 68cm
From an altar (probably a triptych) from
the parish church of St Laurenz in Cologne,
which was secularized in 1803. The
detached outer side with the grisaille
painting of John the Baptist is now in the
Museum of Art in Cleveland. The other
wing, also to be found in the Alte
Pinakothek, shows the Resurrection of Christ
on the inside and John the Evangelist in
grisaille on the outside.
Acquired by King Ludwig I with the
Boisserée collection in 1827. (990)

△
MARY IN THE ROSE BOWER – ST GEORGE
WITH THE DONOR
**Hans Memling (b. Seligenstadt/Main
c 1435/40, d. Bruges 1494), c 1480**
Inside of a diptych
Oak; 43.3 x 31cm (each wing)
The outside of the left wing is unpainted,
that of the right wing has been detached
and shows St Anne with Mary and the
child Jesus. Such diptychs, with portraits
of their donors, were widespread in the
late Middle Ages and served private
devotion. They are thus a testimony to
changing religious feelings at the time.
From the Zweibrücken gallery. (680, 5,
1401)

CHARLES II OF BOURBON AS A CARDINAL
**Jean Hey (working in Burgundy between
1483 and 1501), c 1482/83**
Oak; 34 x 25cm
Third son of Duke Charles I and his wife
Agnes of Burgundy. Appointed Cardinal
in 1476.
Purchased with the Boisserée collection
by King Ludwig I in 1827. (WAF 648)

THE SEVEN JOYS OF MARY

Hans Memling (b. Seligenstadt/Main
c 1435/40, d. Bruges 1494), 1480
Oak; 81 x 189cm
Donated by Pieter Bultnyc and his spouse
Katharina von Riebeke to the chapel of
the tanners in the Frauenkirche in Bruges.
Twenty-five separate incidents from the
story of Mary, including the 'Seven Joys'
(in contrast to the 'Seven sorrows'), and
surely inspired by medieval mystery plays,
are clearly divided over a panoramic
landscape with raised horizon.
In Empress Josephine Beauharnais' collection
in 1804. Purchased by King Ludwig I
with the Boisserée collection in 1827.
(WAF 668)

THE ADORATION OF THE KINGS
**Gerard David (b. Oudewater (Holland)
c 1460, d. Bruges 1523), *c* 1490/95**
Oak; 123 x 166cm

Copy of a lost work by Hugo van der
Goes, probably painted about 1480, in
which the figures are imbued with a new
seriousness.
Purchased by Crown Prince Ludwig from
a private collection in Paris in 1816.
(715)

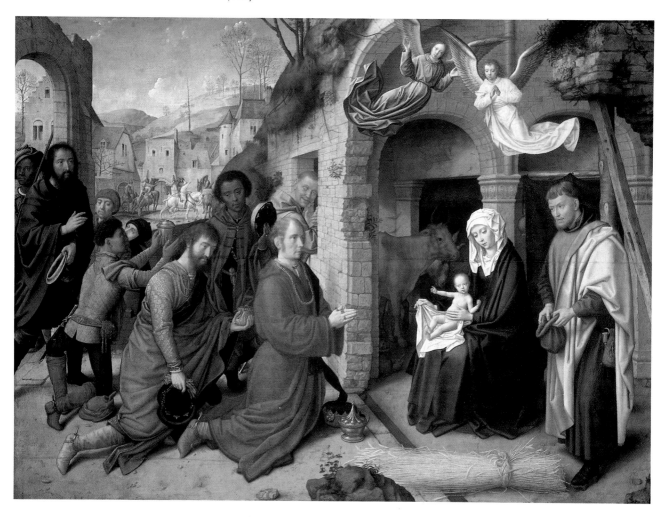

THE LAST JUDGMENT (fragment)
**Hieronymus Bosch (b. 's-Hertogenbosch
c 1450, d. 's-Hertogenbosch 1516),
beginning of 16th century**
Oak; 59.4 x 112.9cm
Fragment (right lower part) of a no
longer traceable large-scale picture of the
Last Judgment which shows the
resurrection of the dead in a fantastic and
surreal manner.
Known to have been in the reserve of the
Filial gallery in the castle at Nüremberg
from 1817 onwards. (5752)

THE REST DURING THE FLIGHT INTO EGYPT
Adriaen Isenbrant (birthplace unknown c 1490, d. Bruges 1551), c 1520/30
Oak; 49.5 x 34cm
The landscape uses suggestions from the Antwerp painter Joachim Patinir, and the figures have been influenced by Gerard David. The childlike, fairy-tale atmosphere, however, reveals Isenbrant's own charming manner of expression.
Purchased by King Ludwig I with the Boisserée collection in 1827. (WAF 398)

THE EMPEROR CONSTANTINE AND ST HELEN
Cornelis Engebrechtsz (b. Leiden (?) c 1460/70, d. Leiden 1527), c 1517 (?)
Oak; 87.5 x 56.5cm (edges trimmed all round)
Presumably a fragment of a larger work (the right wing of a triptych?). It has been supposed that the work was commissioned in connection with a relic of the Holy Cross which found its way to Leiden in 1517. According to legend, Constantine's mother, St Helen, is supposed to have discovered Christ's cross on a pilgrimage to the Holy Land.
From the private gallery of Elector Maximilian I. (1458)

VIRGIN AND CHILD WITH ST MARY MAGDALENE AND DONOR
Lucas van Leyden (b. Leiden probably 1494, d. Leiden 1533), signed and dated 1522
Oak; 50.5 x 67.8cm
Originally a diptych with rounded upper edge, later put together to form a panel and cut across the top. The *Annunciation*, detached from the right wing in 1874, is also in the Alte Pinakothek. The donor was probably changed into St Joseph by the addition of suitable attributes in the early 17th century. The painter has made creative use, in equal measure, of Venetian ideas and Dürer's graphics. According to Van Mander, the painting was in Emperor Rudolf II's collection. From the private gallery of Elector Maximilian I. (742)

ST JEROME
Willem Key (b. Breda *c* 1515,
d. Antwerp 1568), *c* 1550/60
Oak; 147 x 106cm
The painting combines convincingly Flemish
and Italian elements (Michelangelo) in the
context of Netherlandish Romanism.
From the castle in Würzburg. (600)

THE MOCKING OF CHRIST
Jan Sanders van Hemessen (b. Hemixen
near Antwerp *c* 1504, d. Haarlem (?)
before 1567), signed and dated 1544
Oak; 123 x 102.5cm
Typical work of Netherlandish Romanism,
whose realism in the graphic vividness of
facial expression shows the influence of
the physiognomic studies of Leonardo.
From the Düsseldorf gallery. (1408)

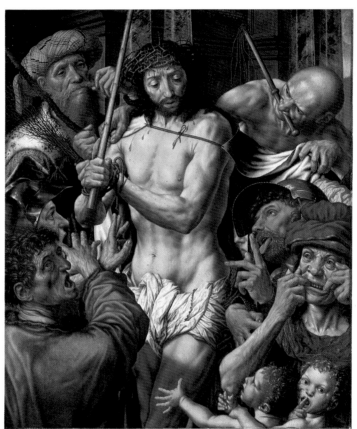

▷
DANAE
Jan Gossaert (b. Maubeuge (Hennegau)
c 1478, d. Breda 1532), signed and
dated 1527
Oak; 113.5 x 95cm
Danae receives the golden rain of Zeus,
which leads to the conception of Perseus.
In contrast to the more sensual treatment
of the theme in the Italian renaissance,
where Danae is shown naked, Gossaert
remains committed to the medieval tradition,
which construed the theme moralistically
as an allegory of chastity.
Known to have been in the Elector's gallery
from 1748 onwards. (38)

A TAX COLLECTOR WITH HIS WIFE

Marinus van Reymerswaele (b. Reymerswael (Zeeland) *c* **1490, d. later than 1497), signed and dated 1538**
Oak; 67 x 103cm

According to the inscription, this is a tax collector named Boisselaer. The painting, which is known in other, only slightly differing, variants, goes back to a picture by Quinten Massys in the Louvre in Paris dated 1514.
From the collection of Elector Maximilian I. (7)

ST CHRISTOPHER

Jan Mandyn (b. Haarlem 1502, d. Antwerp *c* **1560),** *c* **1540/50**
Oak; 142.5 x 179cm

The saint is carrying the Christ child – as described in the *Legenda Aurea* of Jacobus de Vragine – through a torrential river, whose dangers are symbolized by grotesque creatures.
From the Elector's gallery. (690)

Dutch Painting

In 1609 the seven protestant provinces of the northern Netherlands broke away from the catholic provinces in the south, which remained under Spanish suzerainty, to acquire political independence and religious freedom. The development and blossoming of seventeenth-century Dutch painting is closely linked with the emergence of the Republic and the political and economic advances which immediately followed it. This collection of some 1,200 paintings, which is now under the guardianship of the Bavarian State collections and spread over several galleries, must be one of the most extensive in the world. It also owes its emergence to the fact that several lines of Wittelsbachs died out at the turn of the nineteenth century so that in the course of succession, the whole of the Wittelsbach inheritance came under one hand within a few years.

The most important Dutch paintings to be seen in the Alte Pinakothek today come from the Düsseldorf gallery of Elector Johann Wilhelm von der Pfalz. These are Rembrandt's series of pictures of the Passion, which were painted between 1633 and 1639 at the behest of Frederik Hendrik, Governor of the Netherlands. *The descent from the cross* (p.55) is probably one of the early works of the cycle. Two portraits by Ferdinand Bol, which had long ranked as works of Rembrandt, also came from Düsseldorf, as did Jan Steen's *Love-sick girl* (p.65) and *The bean feast* by Gabriel Metsu (p.62), works whose themes appealed particularly to eighteenth-century taste.

Elector Johann Wilhelm, however, was not only a discriminating collector but also an outstanding patron. Like other great art lovers of his time, he was fond of Dutch fine painting and decorative still lifes. So, along with Italian artists, it was mainly Dutch painters that he engaged at his court, such as Egon Hendrik van der Neer, Herman van der Myn and Rachel Ruysch. Adriaen van der Werff, who had been appointed court painter to the Elector in 1696 and raised to noble rank in 1703, was one of the most celebrated artists of his time, overwhelmed with commissions from the royal courts of Europe. Van der Werff's work *The entombment,* which he presented to the Elector in Düsseldorf, gave rise to a whole series of scenes from the life of Christ and the Virgin, while *Children playing in front of a statue of Hercules* (p.68) shows another facet of his work, the moral allegory. Jan Weenix also carried out extensive commissions for Johann Wilhelm, painting for example a series of animal still lifes for the prince's hunting lodge at Bensberg, which were greatly admired and enthusiastically described by Goethe, who saw them while on a journey through the Rhineland in 1774. He is represented here, however, by a human study, the *Sleeping Girl* (p.63).

The Mannheim gallery, built up by the ambitious Elector Karl Philipp (1661-1742) with many a side-glance at the famous treasures of Düsseldorf, found its way to Munich in 1799. It owes its expansion to Karl Philipps' successor, Carl Theodor (1742-1799), who was a lover of art and spectacular display. But whereas the main accent in Düsseldorf had been on Flemish masters, the collectors in Mannheim had chosen predominantly Dutch paintings, which consequently made up the greater part of the 758 pictures in the gallery. From there came the two great Rembrandt paintings, the *Holy Family* (p.56) and the *Sacrifice of Isaac* (p.56), baroque early works dating from the 1630s with special appeal to eighteenth-century taste. Aert de Gelder's splendid *Jewish bride*, which until 1881 had been attributed to Rembrandt, is another of those works of art which demonstrate how zealously the eighteenth century tried to attribute works to this great painter. The delightful *Boy picking fleas from his dog* (p.61) by Gerard ter Borch, which Carl Theodor had brought over from the Düsseldorf gallery, falls — along with Murillo's *Grape and melon eater* (p.92) — into the group of pictures which the 'Savoyard taste' of the *époque galante* revered as precious collectors' items. It is well known that the French court was fond of having the royal children painted in Savoyard costume.

Another expression of *joie de vivre* was found in the peasant and country scenes which reflected the festivals and popular revels of the time and hence were received in large numbers by the gallery. Adriaen van Ostade's peasant pieces like *Peasants making merry in a tavern* (p.58), Jan Steen's *The brawl* and a series of other more famous paintings have never lost their appeal for art lovers since that time. Numerous genre pieces, portraits, landscapes and still lifes are among the works which demonstrate the significance of Mannheim in the building up of the Dutch collection but probably the finest of Carl Theodor's acquisitions was the interior *Woman reading* by Pieter Janssens Elinga (p.64), which was long regarded as being the work of Pieter de Hooch.

The Zweibrücken collection also arrived in Munich in 1799. The youngest of the Wittelsbach galleries, it had been assembled by Duke Karl August (1746-1795) the last reigning prince of the region, for his castle of Carlsberg near Homburg. He acquired the collections of his court painter Christian von Mannlich and of the Palatine court architect Nicolas de Pigage and sent out competent agents to purchase on his behalf the best the market had to offer, especially in Paris. The Alte Pinakothek is indebted to his acquisitions for another work by Rembrandt, the half-length portrait of a *Man in oriental costume* of 1633, whose theme must have appealed to the duke's taste for the unusual. As well as the genre and peasant pieces, landscapes and still lifes which characterise the Dutch section in the Alte Pinakothek today, other pictures were bought in Zweibrücken whose acquisition clearly shows the change in taste towards the end of the century. These include Gabriel Metsu's *The cook* (p.62), a reminder of Chardin's fondness for kitchen scenes, and the forest landscapes by Jacob van Ruysdael and Hobemma, which testify to the English taste for the landscaped park that was taking the continent by storm.

In all, Munich owes its astonishing riches in fine painting and lesser masters to the eighteenth century's ardent love of Dutch seventeenth-century painting. These riches afford a profound insight into the way the Dutch saw and experienced daily life, such as is hardly to be found in this measure in any other collection, except possibly that of the Rijksmuseum in Amsterdam. Munich itself, receiving all these treasures from the other collections around 1800, also already had a considerable collection of Dutch pictures of its own, which were mainly housed in the castle of Schleissheim.

This glorious development of the royal galleries was totally arrested, however, the moment they were united in Munich. Throughout the whole of the nineteenth century Dutch paintings were no longer collected systematically here, unlike other cities which zealously built up their galleries in accordance with new trends in taste. Ludwig I's interests were predominantly directed towards Old German, Old Netherlandish and Italian artists. Nevertheless, when his father Maximilian I's private collection was auctioned in 1826, Ludwig purchased several Dutch pictures, including *Oak trees by a stream* by Jacob van Ruisdael (p.67), the early *Dune landscape* by Philips Wouwerman and *Calm sea* by Willem van de Velde (p.60).

The fact that, in spite of the period of stagnation, the Alte Pinakothek possesses considerable stocks of Dutch Masters, which came to be appreciated only in the 'bourgeois period', is due not so much to the personalities of prominent collectors as to a political phenomenon. As a result of the secularisation in the early nineteenth century precious stocks of paintings, important Dutch works among them, had passed into the hands of the State. Among these were Rembrandt's *Arisen Christ* of 1661 (the only late work of the master in the Alte Pinakothek), no less than five landscapes of Jan van Goyen, Pieter Jansz Saenredam's *Interior of St Jakob's Church, Utrecht* (p.59), Carel Fabritius' *Self portrait* (p.59), a painting by Gerbrand van den Eeckhout, and the magnificent still lifes by Barent van der Meer and Juriaen van Streeck.

It is significant that most of these works were not received into the Alte Pinakothek until this century, when, after an inordinately long time, past omissions were recognised and efforts were made, in spite of limited funds, to fill the gaps. In fact, the two portraits by Ter Borch were purchased in 1901 and the work of Frans Hals, who had never been represented in the gallery before, was introduced in the *Portrait of a man* (p.53), believed to be Willem Croes. In 1927 the collection was enhanced by Philips Koninck's large *Flat landscape* (p.60) and in 1930 the gallery succeeded in purchasing the large group picture *The senior members of the wine merchants' guild,* by Ferdinand Bol (p.63), which came from the collection of King Willem II of the Netherlands and is now one of the rare regency pieces in any gallery outside Holland. In 1940 Ernst Buchner acquired Willem Kalf's significant *Still life* painted in 1653, and in 1953 Eberhard Hanfstaengel purchased the *Self portrait* (p.54) painted by the youthful Rembrandt in 1629. The central painting in the Dutch room is Frans Hals's portrait of Willem van Heythuysen (p.53) purchased by Erich Steingräber in 1969.

A FEAST OF THE GODS
Abraham Blomaert (b. Gorinchem 1564, d. Utrecht 1651), *c* 1595
Canvas; 101 x 146cm
Executed on the model of a copper engraving by Hendrick Goltzius. A typical work of the current international late mannerism which was particularly familiar at the Imperial Court in Prague.
From the Kurmainz gallery in Aschaffenburg. (6526)

ODYSSEUS AND NAUSICAA
Pieter Lastman (b. Amsterdam probably 1583, d. Amsterdam 1633), signed and dated 1619
Oak; 91.5 x 117.2cm
Nausicaa, daughter of King Alcinous, grants the supplication of Odysseus who is stranded off the Phaeacian island of Scheria and entertains him with a display of oriental splendour.
Purchased by Elector Karl Theodor from the Mannheim art dealer De Vigneux in 1792, seized by Napoleonic troops in 1800 and given back in 1815. (4947)

MERRY COMPANY
Gerrit van Honthorst (b. Utrecht 1590, d. Utrecht 1656), signed and dated 1622
Canvas; 130 x 195.6cm
The composition takes its centre and its peculiar theatrically vivid liveliness from the source of light. Honthorst belonged to the group of Utrecht Caravaggians and was nicknamed 'Gherardo delle Notti' in Italy on account of numerous similar pictures.
From the Düsseldorf gallery. (1312)

A TROOPER
Hendrick ter Brugghen (b. near Deventer 1588, d. Utrecht 1629), signed and dated 1627
Canvas; 71.3 x 60cm
Following the model of Caravaggio, the Utrecht painters were fond of painting half figures close to the front edge of the picture and such works had a plastic immediacy. Scenes of loose life like this were intended as a moral admonition.
From the Elector's gallery, Munich. (4845)

GAMES ON THE FROZEN MOAT
Esaias van de Velde (b. Amsterdam *c* 1591, d. The Hague 1630), signed and dated 1618
Oak; 29.8 x 50.4cm
Early example of the new Dutch realistic landscape painting, with folklore-based features.
From the Zweibrücken gallery. (2884)

WILLEM VAN HEYTHUYSEN
Frans Hals (b. Antwerp (?) between
1581 and 1585, d. Haarlem 1666),
c 1625/30
Canvas; 204.5 x 134.5cm
In the proud gait of the obviously wealthy
Haarlem yarn merchant, dressed
according to the latest fashion, the painter
combines the supra-personal aspirations
of the social portrait with the precise
characterization of the individual. The roses
on the floor remind us of the transience of
earthly life.
Acquired from the collection of the Prince
of Liechtenstein in Vaduz in 1969. (14101)

PORTRAIT OF A MAN
Frans Hals (b. Antwerp (?) between
1581 and 1585, d. Haarlem 1666),
signed, c 1660
Oak; 47.1 x 34.4cm
This portrait shows the light, sketch-like,
painterly brushstrokes of the painter's
late works, which make do with a few
shades of the black, grey and brown
range.
Acquired 1906. (8402)

SELF PORTRAIT
Rembrandt Harmensz van Rijn
(b. Leiden 1606, d. Amsterdam 1669),
signed and dated 1629
Oak; 15.5 x 12.7cm
This likeness of the 23-year-old painter
was to be followed by numerous self
portraits in Rembrandt's œuvre, all of
which — in spite of profound artistic changes
— pose the persistent question about the
underlying nature of existence.
Purchased from the family foundation of
the Dukes of Sachsen-Coburg-Gotha in
1953. (11427)

THE DESCENT FROM THE CROSS
Rembrandt Harmensz van Rijn
(b. Leiden 1606, d. Amsterdam 1669),
signed (?), probably 1633
West Indian cedar; 89.4 x 65.2cm
From a series of paintings, loosely held
together by the story of Christ, which
Rembrandt painted for Statthalter (governor)
Frederik Hendrik of Orange. Another five
of the pictures are in the Alte Pinakothek.
The composition drew its inspiration from
the altar picture painted by Rubens for
the Walpurgis church in Antwerp but
Rembrandt's dramatically-lit composition
emphasizes more strongly the human nature
of Christ. Below the figure of Christ the

painter has represented himself.
Purchased by Elector Johann Wilhelm of
the Palatine for the Düsseldorf gallery.
(395)

THE HOLY FAMILY
Rembrandt Harmensz van Rijn
(b. Leiden 1606, d. Amsterdam 1669),
signed and dated *c* 1633
Canvas; 183.5 x 123cm
No other painter before Rembrandt had
humanized the biblical theme in this way.
Purchased by the court painter Lambert
Krahe for the Mannheim gallery in 1760.
(1318)

THE SACRIFICE OF ISAAC
Rembrandt Harmensz van Rijn
(b. Leiden 1606, d. Amsterdam 1669),
signed and dated 1636
Canvas; 195 x 132.3cm
Compared with the similar version in
the Hermitage, Leningrad, painted in 1635,
the dramatic element seems even stronger
here.
Purchased by the Palatine court painter
and gallery director, Lambert Krahe in
1760 for his own collection and later for
the Mannheim gallery. (438)

FARMSTEAD ON THE RIVER
Jan van Goyen (b. Leiden 1596, d.
The Hague 1656), signed and dated
1636
Oak; 39.5 x 60cm
Nature and the work of Man grow together
in an overall greenish-brown tone, which
manages to convey the atmospheric
peculiarities of the Dutch river landscape,
into a harmonious unity.
From the Prince Bishop's gallery in
Würzburg. (4893)

RIVER LANDSCAPE WITH FERRY BOAT
Salomon van Ruysdael (b. Narden
1600/1603, d. Haarlem 1670),
c 1630/35
Oak; 65.6 x 94.4cm
The treatment of this river scene as the
background of the Dutch peasant shows
realism and poetry in equal measure.
From the Elector's gallery in Munich. (161)

STILL LIFE WITH JUG
Pieter Claesz (b. Burgsteinfurt
(Westphalia) *c* 1597, d. Haarlem 1660),
c 1635
Oak; 56 x 86. 5cm
The 'Breakfast Still Life' usually attuned to a
small number of subdued tones, played
an important part in the Dutch painting of
the first half of the 17th century. Several
variants of this painting by the artist himself
are extant.
Purchased from the art-dealer de Vigneux
in Mannheim in 1792. (157)

PEASANTS MAKING MERRY IN A TAVERN
Adriaen van Ostade (b. Haarlem
1610, d. Haarlem 1685), signed,
c 1635
Oak; 28.8 x 36.3cm
The companion piece *Men and Women
in a Peasants' Tavern* is also in the Alte
Pinakothek. Such pictures were painted
for a sophisticated urban public of art
connoisseurs who no longer had any
real connection with the land, nor with the
peasant's way of life, and for that very
reason were attracted by this milieu of
'primitive instincts'.
From the Zweibrücken gallery. (864)

PEASANT REVELRY
Pieter de Bloot (b. Rotterdam 1601,
d. Rotterdam 1658), signed and dated,
probably 1635
Oak; 35.3 x 58.1cm
One of the most popular themes in
Netherlandish painting from Pieter Bruegel
the Elder onwards.
From the Zweibrücken gallery. (6249)

THE SPINNER'S GRACE BEFORE MEAT
Gerard Dou (b. Leiden 1613, d. Leiden
1675), signed, *c* 1645
Oak; 27.7 x 28.3cm
A typical example of Leiden 'Feinmalerei'
(fine painting), this picture illustrates
meticulously the protestant middle-class
virtues of piety and a hard-working family
life.
From the Düsseldorf gallery. (588)

INTERIOR OF ST JACOB'S CHURCH, UTRECHT
Pieter Jansz Saenredam (b. Assendelft
1597, d. Haarlem 1665), signed and
dated 1642
Oak; 55.2 x 43.4cm
The painter's real interest was in the
play of light on the bright, unadorned
plastered walls of the church, which are
reproduced in only one section of the most
brightly lit part of the choir.
From the Prince Bishop's gallery in
Würzburg. (6622)

SELF PORTRAIT
Carel Fabritius (b. Miden-Beemster
(near Amsterdam) 1622, d. Delft 1654),
signed, *c* 1650
Canvas; 62.5 x 51cm (trimmed on all
sides)
The urgent self-questioning on the one
hand, plus the spectacular costumes, remind
us that the painter was trained in
Rembrandt's workshop (1641-1643).
From the Prince Bishop's gallery, Würzburg.
(2080)

△
CALM SEA
Willem van de Velde the Younger
(b. Leiden 1633, d. Westminster 1707),
c 1655
Canvas; 51.6 x 56.5cm
The extremely restrained colour range suits
the dead calm which has brought the
ships to a standstill, giving an impression
of supremely harmonious balance. This
seascape illustrates the importance of
Holland as a sea power.
From King Maximilian I's collection.
(1032)

A BOY PICKING FLEAS FROM HIS DOG
Gerard ter Borch (b. Zwolle 1617,
d. Deventer 1681), *c* 1655
Canvas; 34.4 x 27.1cm
The popularity of this genre picture with
its extremely delicate colours is apparent
from the numerous copies made, even in
the 17th century.
From the Düsseldorf gallery. (589)

LARGE STILL LIFE WITH LOBSTER
Abraham van Beyeren (b. The Hague
1620 or 1621, d. Overschie 1690),
signed and dated 1653
Canvas; 125.5 x 105cm
Sumptuous still lifes of this sort,
exemplifying wealth and abundance, were
popular in Holland in the second half of
the 17th century. The pocket watch reminds
the viewer that time will run out one day,
even for the prosperous citizen.
From the Mannheim gallery. (1620)

◁
FLAT LANDSCAPE
Philips Koninck (b. Amsterdam 1619,
d. Amsterdam 1688), *c* 1650/55
Canvas; 133.3 x 165.7cm
A wide, flat, Dutch landscape with a low
horizon, in which the overcast sky
stands out as the main element.
Purchased from art dealers in Munich
1927. (9407)

▷
WINTER LANDSCAPE WITH ICE
Philips Wouverman (b. Haarlem 1619,
d. Haarlem 1668), signed, 1655/60
Oak; 47.5 x 63.7cm
Popular amusements on ice are among the
favourite themes of Dutch genre painting.
The white horse is nearly always present
in Wouverman's work.
From the Zweibrücken gallery. (152)

THE BEAN FEAST
Gabriel Metsu (b. Leiden 1629,
d. Amsterdam 1667), *c* 1650/55
Canvas; 80.9 x 97.9cm
The one who found a bean hidden in the
cake on Twelfth Night, a popular
Netherlandish festival, was crowned the
Bean King. Occasionally the Kingship
also fell to him by lot and this was then
pinned to the paper crown as in this
picture.
From the Düsseldorf gallery. (871)

THE COOK
Gabriel Metsu (b. Leiden 1629,
d. Amsterdam 1667), signed, *c* 1665
Oak; 28.7 x 23.9cm
The Leiden 'Feinmaler' (fine painters),
particularly Gerard Dou, to whom Metsu's
late work is indebted, liked portraying
servant girls and female cooks in half-length,
illustrating the prosperous domestic culture
of the Dutch middle class.
From the Zweibrücken gallery. (624)

THE SENIOR MEMBERS OF THE WINE
MERCHANTS' GUILD
**Ferdinand Bol (b. Dordrecht 1616,
d. Amsterdam 1680), probably 1659**
Canvas; 193.5 x 305cm
Group portraits of august guilds and
members of the governing body were among
the best paid commissions of Dutch
painters in the 17th century. Probably
painted in the foundation year of the
Amsterdam wine merchants guild in 1659.
In the possession of King Willem II of
the Netherlands until 1850. Purchased in
1930. (9656)

SLEEPING GIRL
**Jan Baptist Weenix (b. Amsterdam
1621, d. Huis ter May (near Utrecht)
c 1660), signed and dated 1656**
Canvas; 66 x 54cm
Among the Schildersbent or Bentvueghels,
a group of Netherlandish artists in Rome,
the painter found his own style, which
was deeply influenced by the bright
Southern light.
From the Düsseldorf gallery. (869)

WOMAN READING
Pieter Janssens Elinga (b. Bruges 1632, d. Amsterdam 1682), *c* **1660**
Canvas; 75.5 x 63.5cm
The light-suffused interior conveys quietness, comfort and security but also the widespread prosperity of the Dutch middle class in the 17th century.
Purchased from the art-dealer de Vigneux in Mannheim in 1791. (284)

THE LOVE-SICK GIRL
**Jan Steen (b. Leiden 1625 or 1626,
d. Leiden 1679),** *c* 1660
Canvas; 61 x 52.1cm
In the love-sick girl's hand there is a slip
of paper with the text 'Daar baat geen
medesyn, want het is minepyn' (Against
love-sickness no medicine can help).
From the Düsseldorf gallery. (158)

THE SICK GOAT
Karel Dujardin (probably b. Amsterdam *c* 1620, d. Venice 1678), signed, *c* 1665
Canvas; 84.5 x 73cm
The anecdotal title was given to the picture only in the 19th century. To this day it has not been possible to interpret precisely its actual content, no doubt tinged with eroticism.
From the Mannheim gallery. (291)

LADY AT THE MIRROR
Frans van Mieris (b. Leiden 1635, d. Leiden 1681), *c* 1670
Canvas; 43 x 31.5cm
The mirror, symbol of vanity, reminds the gay young lady of the transience of all earthly things.
From the Elector's gallery. (219)

THE OLD PALACE IN BRUSSELS
Jan van der Heyden (b. Gorinchem (Gorkum) 1637, d. Amsterdam 1712), signed, *c* 1665
Oak; 50.8 x 63.5cm
A topographically accurate architectural veduta. The palace served as a residence for the sovereigns (also for the Bavarian Elector Max Emanuel when he was governor of the Netherlands).
From the castle gallery in Ansbach. (7287)

VIEW OF OOTMARSUM
Jacob van Ruisdael (b. Haarlem 1628
or 1629, d. Amsterdam (?) 1682),
with false signature, c 1670/75
Canvas; 59.1 x 73.2cm
A broad, flat landscape with allusions to
the human scene dominated by God
and the elements.
Purchased from the collection of Prince
Ernst von Sachsen-Meiningen, 1942.
(10818)

OAK TREES BY A STREAM
Jacob van Ruisdael (b. Haarlem 1628
or 1629, d. Amsterdam (?) 1682),
signed (?), c 1670/80
Canvas mounted on oak wood;
71.7 x 90.1cm
The depiction of Nature, powerful yet full
of pathos, holds in antithesis numerous
allusions to transience and permanence.
From the estate of King Max I, who
purchased the picture from the Count Fries
collection in Vienna in 1815. (1038)

▷

ITALIAN LANDSCAPE IN THE EVENING LIGH
**Nicolas Berchem (b. Haarlem 1620, c
Amsterdam 1683), signed, *c* 1670/75**
Oak; 41.2 x 54.5cm
Alongside Claude Lorrain, it was the
Dutch Italianists who introduced into
Northern painting the conception of a war
sun-drenched landscape.
From the Elector's gallery. (266)

FAMILY PORTRAIT
**Emanuel de Witte (b. Alkmaar
1616/18, d. Amsterdam 1692), signe
and dated 1678**
Canvas; 68.5 x 86.5cm
Here the painter, who is chiefly famous fo
his church interiors, gives a portrait of
the rich Dutch bourgeoisie in the 17th
century, with its strict Protestant morality
Purchased by the Friends of the Alte
Pinakothek in 1972. (FV 2)

CHILDREN PLAYING IN FRONT OF A STATU
OF HERCULES
**Adriaen van der Werff (b. Kralingen,
near Rotterdam, 1659, d. Rotterdam
1722), signed and dated 1687**
Oak; (with rounded top edge) 46.8 x
35cm
This picture, to be interpreted as a
moral allegory, could also be entitled 'In
praise of virtue and down with vice'.
From the Düsseldorf gallery. (250)

◁
ESTHER BEFORE GOING TO AHASUERUS
Aert de Gelder (b. Dordrecht 1645, d. Dordrecht 1727), signed and dated 1684
Canvas; 139.4 x 163.3cm
Esther, the wife of the Persian king Ahasuerus, valiantly rescued her Jewish companions in the faith from sore oppression and hence passed into history as one of the great figures of ancient times (Old Testament: Book of Esther). Although the fashion is that of late 17th century Europe, the impression is nevertheless one of oriental splendour. From the Mannheim gallery. (841)

Flemish Painting

One of the most important departments in the Alte Pinakothek is that of the Flemish school, particularly the seventeenth century, whose focal point is the Rubens collection, one of the greatest anywhere in the world. This unique group did not come together solely as the result of the collecting zeal of later generations: its nucleus goes back to commissions given to Rubens by the Bavarian princes and bishops, and it should be borne in mind that Elector Maximilian I and his brother-in-law, Wolfgang Wilhelm von der Pfalz Neuburg, were the only German princes for whom Rubens carried out commissions.

In 1616 he painted the cycle of four hunting pictures for Maximilian to decorate the old castle of Schleissheim; after their seizure in the Napoleonic wars, only one of these, *The hippopotamus and crocodile hunt* (p.78) returned to Munich. In 1616/19, commissioned by Wolfgang Wilhelm, Rubens painted the altar pictures for the newly built Jesuit church in Neuburg on the Danube, among them the famous *'Large' Last judgment.* These pictures did not find their way to Munich directly but first went to Düsseldorf to the gallery which a grandson of Wolfgang Wilhelm, Elector Johann Wilhelm von der Pfalz, who had been in power since 1690, was building up with the utmost enthusiasm.

Johann Wilhelm's interest was directed not only to Italian and Dutch masters but especially to the Flemish school, and he brought together as many as forty-six pictures bearing the name of Rubens. He seems to have begun collecting as early as 1684, that is to say six years before he acceded to his high office. There is, however, an old anecdote (unfortunately contradicted by the archives), according to which he, as an already reigning prince, is supposed to have been seduced into collecting pictures by the guile of his court painter Douven, who by stealth hung the *Battle of the Amazons* in his dining-room.

How the *Battle of the Amazons* (p.79), which is today one of the most important and best known pictures in the Pinakothek, came into Johann Wilhelm's possession we do not know. In Rubens' lifetime it was in the collection of his patron, the Antwerp businessman Cornelis van der Geest, and later in the possession of the Duke de Richelieu.

Johann Wilhelm seems to have maintained innumerable contacts with various agents in the Netherlands, so that he could buy pictures by Rubens at every opportunity—according to contemporary reports, the prices of Rubens' paintings rose by more than half as a result of his zeal. Some of the pictures were purchased directly from churches without the need for negotiations with private collectors, although this was not without hard bargaining, in the course of which Johann Wilhelm often had to undertake to provide copies or replacements in the form of other paintings. Johann Wilhelm's tenacity in pursuing his goals is demonstrated by the efforts he made over many years to incorporate the pictures commissioned by his grandfather for the church of the Jesuits in

Neuburg into his gallery in Düsseldorf. In the case of the *'Large' Last Judgment* not too much effort seems to have been needed to persuade the authorities to release the painting — apparently because of its 'offensive nudity' — for it reached Düsseldorf as early as 1692, but it was only in 1703, after Rome had given permission and Johann Wilhelm had promised to replace them, that it was possible to transfer the other two pictures.

The Düsseldorf collection was publicised at an early date. J.G. Karsch, the curator of the gallery at the time, compiled the first printed catalogue in 1719, while the great work on the gallery by Nicolas de Pigage, the Palatine court architect and landscape gardener, appeared in 1778. Among the illustrations there are reproductions of whole walls hung with pictures in all five halls of the gallery. The pictures scattered in the side rooms are described by Johan van Gool in a work on Netherlandish painters which appeared in the Hague in 1751. As a result of this unusually early published documentation the Düsseldorf gallery was strongly imprinted on the consciousness of art-lovers all over the world. Johann Jakob Heinse's 'Letters from the Düsseldorf Gallery', published in 1776/77, containing descriptions of Rubens' pictures which were of special importance for the history of his literary pieces, also lent decisive significance to the Düsseldorf collection by the impetus it gave to the development of the history of art as a scientific discipline.

When the Rubens pictures finally came to Munich at the end of a war-imposed odyssey in 1806 and were united with the stocks of the other Wittelsbach princes, the collection here actually afforded the most complete and most accessible view of Rubens' œuvre for the critical studies on art history which were developing in Germany in the nineteenth century.

The fame of the Düsseldorf gallery often leads us to forget that many quite important paintings by Rubens came to Munich, along with other Flemish pictures, from a different source, namely the Elector's gallery at Schleissheim. These included the sixteen sketches for the Medici cycle first mentioned in 1729, *The massacre of the innocents* (p.82) and *Meleager and Atalanta* (p.82). It is not clear when either of these paintings came to Schleissheim or from where, but in the case of one group of twelve of his paintings we do have more exact information. They were among the 101 paintings purchased by Elector Max Emanuel in 1698 from the Netherlandish merchant Gisbert van Colen. It is possible that through a relationship with the Fourment family — Fourment was the family name of Rubens' second wife Hélène — Van Colen was able to gain possession of private Rubens pictures, which Rubens had never intended for sale but always kept in his own house, including the four portraits of Hélène. These family testaments took their place beside other pictures from the private sphere of Rubens' life: the self portrait with his first wife Isabella Brant, the famous *Honeysuckle bower* (p.77) from Düsseldorf, and the wonderful portrait of his father-in-law Jan Brant, which Max Emanuel had purchased from another source in Belgium.

The purchase from Gisbert van Colen represented a most valuable enrichment of the total Flemish stocks. Van Dyck's splendid double portrait of the painter Jan de Wael and his wife was also part of it, as well as the portrait of a woman and child thought to be the wife of the painter Theodor Rombouts (p.84). They were added to the great collection, mainly from Düsseldorf, of portraits and religious pictures by Van Dyck, the most important seventeenth-century Flemish painter after Rubens.

A special treasure in the Van Colen purchase are the seven paintings by Adriaen Brouwer, including the *Peasants smoking and drinking* (p.86) and *Peasants playing cards in a tavern* (p.85) which, together with paintings from the Mannheim and Zweibrücken galleries and other electoral possessions in Munich, make up the incomparable Brouwer collection in the Alte Pinakothek. This group of seventeen masterpieces by the brilliant painter of peasant life, which were already much sought after even his lifetime, is by far the most extensive anywhere.

The name of Jan Brueghel, the second eldest son of Pieter Bruegel the Elder, and a collaborator of Rubens, should also be mentioned in this collection. The rich stock of thirty paintings, mainly from the Elector's and the Mannheim galleries, is probably not only the largest but with its fresh, exquisite pictures also one of the finest groups by this master, whose flower pieces and landscapes — such as *Landscape with windmills* (p.75) — have long been highly thought of by collectors throughout Europe.

The transfer of the various Wittelsbach galleries to Munich at the end of the eighteenth and the beginning of the nineteenth centuries increased the Flemish department of the Alte Pinakothek to its present size. Only a few individual pictures have been added. In 1804, in the course of the secularisation, Rubens' high altar picture from the cathedral of Freising, *The apocalyptic woman*, came to Munich. Commissioned by the Prince Bishop of Freising and painted around 1624/25, this work accords well with the other religious pictures from Neuburg.

With the acquisition of *The Land of Cockaigne* (p.74) in 1917, Pieter Bruegel the Elder, the most important Flemish painter of the sixteenth century, was at last fittingly represented in the Alte Pinakothek. For centuries his pictures had been accorded the highest acclaim — by Rubens, among others — and had also ranked among the greatest rarities right from the time when Emperor Rudolf, from whose collection the Munich picture had originally come, had been almost fanatical in buying them up. *The Land of Cockaigne* is now the focal point of a collection whose source was mainly the Munich electoral possessions and which also embraces works by Bruegel's manneristic Antwerp contemporaries such as Jan van Hemessen and Marinus van Roymerswaele.

LANDSCAPE WITH FARMSTEAD
Cornelis van Dalem (b. Antwerp (?)
c 1530/35, d. Breda (?) 1573), **signed**
and dated 1564
Oak; 103 x 127.5cm

The impression made by this painting
is surprisingly unconventional and modern
on account of the unpretentious subject
matter, which is sublimated exclusively by
the pictorial treatment with its strong
emotional appeal.
Purchased from a private owner in Munich
in 1954. (12044)

THE LAND OF COCKAIGNE
Pieter Bruegel the Elder (b. Breda (?) c 1525, d. Brussels 1569), signed and dated 1566
Oak; 52 x 78cm
As Hans Sachs has pointed out, worry and toil are unknown in the Land of Cockaigne, just as they are in Hesiod's Golden Age, in Virgil's Arcadian fields and in the Garden of Eden. Yet the moral warning must not be overlooked: gluttony and drunkenness, in which all ranks indulge, lead to sloth and apathy. Purchased in 1917: formerly in the Imperial collection in Prague, from which it was taken by the Swedes in 1648. (8940)

▷
LANDSCAPE WITH WINDMILLS
Jan Brueghel the Elder (b. Brussels 1568, d. Antwerp 1625), signed and dated 1611
Copper; 9.5 x 15cm
From the Mannheim gallery. (1892)

HARBOUR WITH CHRIST PREACHING
Jan Brueghel the Elder (b. Brussels
1568, d. Antwerp 1625), signed and
dated 1598
Oak; 78 x 119cm

Around 1600 Brueghel was painting
panoramic 'world landscapes' with an
abundance of figures and with raised
horizons, before going over to the new
portrait-like conception of landscape of
the 17th century which is to be seen in his
Landscape with Windmills.
From the Mannheim gallery. (187)

▷
RUBENS AND ISABELLA BRANT IN THE
HONEYSUCKLE BOWER
Peter Paul Rubens (b. Siegen
(Westphalia) 1577, d. Antwerp 1640),
c 1609/10
Canvas mounted on wood; 178 x 136.5cm
On 3 October 1609, Rubens married
the eighteen-year-old daughter of the
Antwerp patrician and City Clerk Jan Brant.
Honeysuckle has been a well-known symbol
of married love since the Middle Ages,
and the linked right hands are also
indicative of the married state. This early
work of the master—one of the most
tender marriage portraits in the history of
art—was probably originally intended
for the bride's parents.
From the Düsseldorf gallery. (334)

◁
OLYMPUS
Abraham Janssens (b. Antwerp
1573/74, d. Amsterdam 1632), *c* 1620
Canvas; 207 x 240cm
Venus, denounced by Hera, is defending
herself before Zeus and the court of the
Gods. Janssens' coming to terms with
Caravaggio's *verismo* is evident, just as
it is in the early Rubens, in the buxom
solidity of the figures.
From the Elector's gallery in Munich. (4884)

SATYR IN THE PEASANT'S HOUSE
Jacob Jordaens (b. Antwerp 1593,
d. Antwerp 1678), after 1620
Canvas on oak; 174 x 205cm
From *Aesop's Fables* (LXXIV). Jordaens
went back repeatedly to this theme. The
lively *verismo* treats Caravaggio's
revolutionary art in a native Flemish
manner.
From the Düsseldorf gallery. (425)

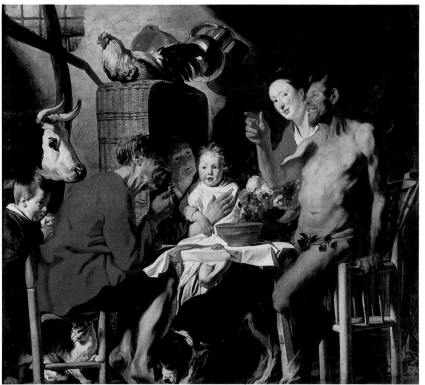

POLDER LANDSCAPE WITH HERD OF COWS
Peter Paul Rubens (b. Siegen (Westphalia) 1577, d. Antwerp 1640), *c* 1618/20
Oak; 81 x 106cm
The fertile Flemish soil found its highest artistic expression in Rubens' polder landscapes.
Purchased by Elector Max Emanuel from the Antwerp tradesman Gisbert van Colen in 1698, in a lot of 101 mostly Flemish paintings, amongst which were twelve by Rubens. (322)

▷
'SMALL' LAST JUDGMENT
Peter Paul Rubens (b. Siegen (Westphalia) 1577, d. Antwerp 1640), *c* 1620
Oak; with rounded upper edge, 183 x 120cm
Based on the account in Matthew: 24, 30-32, 25, 31-46, this picture is akin to the slightly earlier *'Large' Last Judgment*, also in the Alte Pinakothek.
From the Düsseldorf gallery. (611)

LANDING IN MARSEILLES (3.11.1600)
Peter Paul Rubens (b. Siegen (Westphalia) 1577, d. Antwerp 1640), *c* 1621/22
Sketch for the Medici Cycle
Oak; 64 x 50cm
Maria de' Medici was married to King Henry IV of France in October 1600 and after his assassination, on 14 May 1610, she conducted the business of state for the Dauphin who was still a minor. The paintings cycle executed for the Palais du Luxembourg, which was built between 1612 and 1620 (the twenty-one monumental paintings completed in 1625 are in the Louvre), is one of the most significant secular apotheoses of the Baroque period. The Alte Pinakothek has sixteen coloured sketches, others are in the Hermitage in Leningrad.
From the Elector's gallery in Schleissheim. (95)

THE MASSACRE OF THE INNOCENTS
Peter Paul Rubens (b. Siegen (Westphalia) 1577, d. Antwerp 1640),
c 1635/40
Oak; 199 x 302cm

The cruel spectacle receives its most heightened dramatic treatment in this artistically presented late work.
Purchased by Elector Max Emanuel for the Schleissheim gallery before 1706. (572)

MELEAGER AND ATALANTA
Peter Paul Rubens (b. Siegen (Westphalia) 1577, d. Antwerp 1640),
c 1635
Canvas; 199 x 153cm (with later addition, folded-over, on the right)
The beautiful Arcadian huntress Atalanta and the king's son Meleager, who together successfully pursued the raging Caledonian wild boar, are brought together by Cupid. The figure of Moira in the sky, however, points to the tragic outcome of this ancient love story.
From the Elector's gallery in Schleissheim. (355)

HELÈNE FOURMENT IN HER WEDDING DRESS
Peter Paul Rubens (b. Siegen
Westphalia) 1577, d. Antwerp 1640),
1630/31
Oak; 163.5 x 136.9cm
The artist's second wife, daughter of an
Antwerp merchant, whom he married

on 6 December 1630, is represented as a
sixteen-year-old bride in a sumptuous
brocade dress, a head-dress set with pearls
and jewels, and all the other requisites
of a princely baroque portrait.
Purchased by Elector Max Emanuel from
Gisbert van Colen in 1698. (340)

THE REST DURING THE FLIGHT INTO EGYPT
Sir Anthony van Dyck (b. Antwerp 1599, d. London 1641), *c* **1627/32**
Canvas; 134.7 x 114.8cm
The exceptional humanization of the religious theme makes this picture one of the most popular exhibits in the Alte Pinakothek. The encounter with Venetian painting is unmistakable. Probably painted for Brother Theodor, a Canon of St Michael's church in Antwerp.
Purchased by Elector Max Emanuel. (555)

THE WIFE OF THE PAINTER THEODOR ROMBOUTS AND HER DAUGHTER (?)
Sir Anthony van Dyck (b. Antwerp 1599, d. London 1641), *c* **1632**
Oak; 122.8 x 90.7cm
Companion piece to the portrait of the painter Theodor Rombouts (?), also in the Alte Pinakothek.
Purchased by Elector Max Emanuel from Gisbert van Colen in 1698. (599)

THE PAINTER JAN DE WAEL AND HIS WIFE GERTRUD DE JODE
Sir Anthony van Dyck (b. Antwerp 1599, d. London 1641), between 1627 and 1632
Canvas; 125.3 x 139.7cm
Although no authenticated paintings of the once-esteemed Antwerp painter are now known, Van Dyck has created here, with fine psychological intuition, one of the most impressive portraits of a married couple in European baroque painting.
Purchased by Elector Max Emanuel from Gisbert van Colen in 1698. (596)

BANQUET AT THE HOUSE OF
BÜRGERMEISTER ROCKOX
Frans II Francken (b. Antwerp 1581,
d. Antwerp 1642), signed 1630/35
Oak; 62.3 x 96.5cm
This portrait of the *Kunstkammer* (art gallery)
belonging to the prosperous Bürgermeister
gave the painter the opportunity to represent
at the same time the five senses: hearing
(lute player), sight (man with spectacles),
smell (woman smelling a flower), taste
(wine drinker), and touch (people warming
themselves at the fireplace).
From the Düsseldorf gallery. (858)

PEASANTS PLAYING CARDS IN A TAVERN
Adriaen Brouwer (b. Oudenaarde
1605/06, d. Antwerp 1638), *c* 1631/32
Oak; 33 x 43cm

Brouwer's genre scenes, much admired
by Rubens and whose clay-like colours
gave rise to a school in the 19th century,
not only portray the everyday lives of
Flemish peasants but also, with their
allusions to the evils of gambling, drinking
and gluttony, have a pervading moral
content.
Purchased by Elector Max Emanuel from
Gisbert van Colen in 1698. (218)

COW PASTURE WITH SLEEPING WOMAN
Jan Siberechts (b. Antwerp 1627, d. London 1703), after 1660
Canvas; 107 x 83cm
The cool, silvery colour and the intimacy of the detail anticipate features which were again to characterize the landscape painting of the French realists only around the middle of the 19th century.
From the Zweibrücken gallery. (2165)

△
PEASANTS SMOKING AND DRINKING
Adriaen Brouwer (b. Oudenaarde 1605/06, d. Antwerp 1638), c 1635
Oak; 35 x 26cm
Purchased by Elector Max Emanuel from Gisbert van Colen in 1698. (2062)

STILL LIFE WITH FLOWERS, CRUCIFIX AND SKULL
Jan Davidsz de Heem (b. Utrecht 1606, d. Antwerp (?) 1683/84)
and
Nicolaes van Veerendael (b. Antwerp 1640, d. Antwerp 1691) signed, c 1665
Canvas; 103 x 85cm
The *vanitas* still life warns us of the transience of all earthly things and promises resurrection through Christ's death on the cross.
Purchased by Elector Max Emanuel from Gisbert van Colen in 1698. (568)

Spanish Painting

With just twenty-two paintings, the Spanish section in the Alte Pinakothek is the smallest, but also one of the most complete, because every important master is represented. The oldest paintings in the collection are the portraits of Albrecht the Pious and his consort, the Infanta Clara Eugenia of Spain, painted by Pantoja de la Cruz in 1600, which found their way to Munich from the monastery of Hohenwart in 1804 as a result of the secularisation, and the *Disrobing of Christ* by El Greco (p.88), which was purchased by Hugo von Tschudi in 1909. Elector Max Emanuel bought two genre pictures by Murillo in Antwerp when he was Spanish governor of the Netherlands — one, *The grape and melon eater* (p.92) as early in 1691 and the other, *Boys playing with dice,* in 1698 — and thus laid the foundations of the famous set of Murillos in Munich. The addition to the Murillo collection of *The little fruit-seller* and *Domestic grooming* (p.92) in the reign of Elector Maximilian III Josef (1727-1777) was due to the generosity of court chamberlain Franz Joseph von Dufresne, who left these works to the gallery in 1768. Zurbarán's *St Francis in ecstasy* (p.93), Ribera's *St Peter of Alcántara* and the fifth of Murillo's genre pictures, *The pastry-eaters,* came to Munich with the Mannheim gallery. The fact that a painting by Zurbarán found its way into a gallery outside Spain as early as the eighteenth century is unusual, since this painter did not gain European recognition until the nineteenth century, but in fact the purchase was due to an error: the *St Francis* was thought to be a major work by Guido Reni.

From the Düsseldorf gallery came the *Young Spanish nobleman* by Velazquez (p.91), which had been purchased by Elector Johann Wilhelm. Along with his contemporary Elector Max Emanuel, he was one of the first to include Spanish pictures in his collections. King Max I of Bavaria not only united the various Wittelsbach collections in one gallery, but also made considerable sums of money available for new acquisitions. As a result, Crown Prince Ludwig, with Johann Georg von Dillis as his adviser, was able to purchase three important paintings in Paris for the Spanish collection: *St Peter of Alcántara walking over the Guadiana River* by Claudio Coello and *The Virgin appearing to St Anthony* by Alonso Cano (p.90). The latest addition to the Spanish room, in 1984, was Zurbarán's *The entombment of St Catherine of Alexandria on Mount Sinai,* (p.93) which dates from about 1636.

THE DISROBING OF CHRIST

El Greco (Doménikos Theotokópolous:
b. Candia, Crete, 1541, d. Toledo
1614), c 1590/1600
Canvas; 165 x 99cm
The painting, treating the theme in a
powerfully spiritual way, follows the
description in the apocryphal gospel of
Nicodemus. This was the third independent
version of the theme: El Greco made the
first for the sacristy of the cathedral in
Toledo.
Purchased from French art dealers in
1909 (Tschudi Donation). (8573)

THE INFANTA CLARA EUGENIA OF SPAIN

Juan Pantoja de la Cruz (b. Valladolid
1553, d. Madrid 1608), signed and
dated 1599
Canvas; 125 x 97cm
Companion piece to the portrait of Albrecht
the Pious, Archduke of Austria, both
wedding portraits in accordance with the
strict etiquette of the 'Spanish fashion'.
Acquired in 1804 when the Benedictine
monastery of Hohenwart was secularized.
(898)

ST BARTHOLOMEW
José de Ribera (b. Játiva (Valencia) 1591, d. Naples 1652), *c* 1633/35
Canvas; 76 x 64cm
In spite of the crude *verismo* in the style of his model Caravaggio, Ribera's saints have a highly ascetic and spiritual look. Purchased by King Max II in 1861 from the estate of the gallery curator Gündter in Munich. (7604)

THE VIRGIN APPEARING TO ST ANTHONY
Alonso Cano (b. Granada 1601, d. Granada 1667), *c* 1645/52
Canvas; 161 x 111cm
St Anthony (d. 1231 in Padua), is here represented in the robes of a Portuguese Franciscan monk.
Purchased by King Max I in 1815 from the estate of the Empress Josephine Beauharnais, wife of the Emperor Napoleon I. (993)

YOUNG SPANISH NOBLEMAN
**Diego Rodriguez de Silva y Velazquez
(b. Seville 1599, d. Madrid 1660),
probably between 1623 and 1630**
Canvas; 89 x 69cm

Unfinished: only the head, collar and
background have been worked. The
still-perceptible influence of Caravaggio is
subordinated to tonal values of black,
grey and shades of brown, a typical feature
of the mature work of Velazquez.
Purchased in Madrid by Elector Wilhelm
of the Palatine in 1694 for the Düsseldorf
gallery. (518)

91

ST THOMAS OF VILLANUEVA HEALING A
LAME MAN
Bartolomé Esteban Murillo (b. Seville
1618, d. Seville 1682), c 1670/80
Canvas; 221 x 149cm
The Augustine hermit, active in the 16th
century, was greatly revered in Spain as

a friend of the poor and the sick. Painted
for the monastery church of St Augustine
in Seville along with its companion piece
St Thomas as a Child Distributing his
Clothes (Cincinnati Museum).
Purchased in 1815 by King Max I from
General Sebastiani in Paris. (52)

DOMESTIC GROOMING
Bartolomé Esteban Murillo (b. Seville
1618, d. Seville 1682), c 1670/75
Canvas; 147 x 113cm
Purchased in 1768 by Elector Max III
Joseph from the estate of Kammerrat
(Councillor of the Chamber) Franz Joseph
von Dufresne in Munich. (489)

THE GRAPE AND MELON EATER
Bartolomé Esteban Murillo (b. Seville
1618. d. Seville 1682), c 1645/46
Canvas; 146 x 104cm
Like Caravaggio before him in Italy, Murillo
began by exploring the vida picaresca of
the vagabond rascals of Seville. With
five paintings, Munich has the finest
collection of such genre pictures, which
Murillo only painted occasionally and
which had already become rare in the
18th century.
Probably purchased by Elector Max
Emanuel in 1698 during his period as
governor in the Netherlands. (605)

OLD HAWKER WOMAN
Bartolomé Esteban Murillo (b. Seville 1618, d. Seville 1682), *c* **1640/45**
Canvas; 79.1 x 63.5cm
Formerly designated as being the work of J. Ribera, the veristic conception of this Sevillian folk-figure is closer to the early Murillo.
From the Mannheim gallery. (608)

△
ST FRANCIS IN ECSTASY
Francisco Zurbarán y Salazar (b. Fuente de Cantos (Estremadura) 1598, d. Madrid 1664), *c* **1660**
Canvas; 65 x 53cm
This rendering of the saint, in his Capuchin habit, in mystical ecstasy follows a scheme prevailing since the Council of Trent. In his late works, Zurbarán's austere style of painting shows a softening under the influence of Murillo's more genial palate.
From the Mannheim gallery. (504)

THE ENTOMBMENT OF ST CATHERINE OF ALEXANDRIA ON MOUNT SINAI
Francisco Zurbarán y Salazar (b. Fuente de Cantos (Estremadura) 1598, d. Madrid 1664), *c* **1637**
Canvas; 201.5 x 126cm
This altarpiece, painted for the Chapel of St Catherine in the church of San José in Seville, was in France from the time of the Napoleonic War until 1810. It comes from Zurbarán's period of greatest creativity, of which the 'mystical style' is most characteristic, uniting the everyday and earthly with the heavenly in sublime fashion.

STUDIO SCENE
Claudio José Vicente Antolinez
(b. Madrid 1635, d. Madrid 1675),
c 1670
Canvas; 202 x 126cm
Perhaps originally the official name-plate of
an art dealer.
A present from the artist Sigmund Röhrer
in 1909. (8577)

STILL LIFE WITH MELONS, QUINCES AND
PEARS
Luis Meléndez (b. Naples 1716, d.
Madrid 1780), signed c 1765/70
Canvas; 50 x 37cm
This still life was not conceived as an
artistically composed show-piece as in
the Netherlands, but shows — absolutely in
line with the older Spanish tradition of
the Bodegón — a few everyday fruits which
are realistic in their unique form. (13199)

French Painting

The collecting zeal of the various lines of the Wittelsbach dynasty, with its main concentration on early German, Netherlandish and Italian painting, led to the Alte Pinakothek becoming one of the most important galleries in the world. Strangely enough, none of the Bavarian nor the Palatine electors collected French paintings to any great extent, in spite of the ties of blood and also the political links they had with France. Thus the French section has remained the smallest after the Spanish in the Bavarian State collections. About one tenth of the whole collection of some 400 pictures is on display in the Alte Pinakothek.

The Wittelsbachs residing in Munich only occasionally purchased works by French masters. For example, in the reign of Elector Ferdinand Maria (1636-1679) two paintings by Claude Lorrain joined the collection, namely *Seaport with rising sun* (p.99) and *Idyllic landscape at sunset,* both of which had been in the possession of the imperial counsellor Baron Franz von Mayer of Regensburg. *The Roman lime-kiln* by Sebastien Bourdon, which was probably purchased later, also came from the Von Mayer source. Three other pictures by Poussin are not recorded in the inventories until the middle of the eighteenth century — the *Lamentation, Midas and Bacchus* and *Apollo and Daphne.* Mention is made of Bourdon's *Perseus and Andromeda* in the Badenburg in Nymphenburg as early as 1751, and of *The small crown of thorns* and *Erminia among the shepherds* by Valentin de Boulogne (p.97) around the same time in the Munich Residenz. Between 1706 and 1712, and again from 1716 onwards, Joseph Vivien was employed as court painter to Elector Max Emanuel. He was the source of a series of important paintings which, apart from the portrait of Archbishop Fénelon were exhibited in the State gallery in Schleissheim Castle. In spite of very close ties with France, Max Emanuel did not purchase any notable paintings of the French school. On the other hand, his expensive acquisitions of Flemish and Dutch masters made Schleissheim one of the most significant galleries in Europe.

The Zweibrücken collection was the latest Wittelsbach gallery to be brought to Munich, in 1799. As the old stocks had been auctioned in Paris in 1755, Duke Karl August (1746-1795), whose reign had begun in the same year, felt obliged to lay in new ones. First he purchased the collection of his court painter, Christian von Mannlich, who later became director of the Munich gallery, and then that of the Palatine court architect, Nicolas de Pigage. In barely twenty years the stocks had grown to 2,000 pictures, and special rooms had to be built for them in Carlsberg Castle. From Mannlich's collection came the two famous pictures by Claude Lorrain, *The repudiation of Hagar* (p.99) and *Hagar and Ismael in the wilderness.* Some notable eighteenth-century French paintings also came to Munich for the first time via the Zweibrücken gallery, among them Boucher's *Girl resting* (p.104), Chardin's *Woman scraping vegetables* (p.102), the portrait of the Count Palatine Michael von Zweibrücken-Birkenfeld by Louis Tocqué, works by Le Moine and Charles Antoine Coypel and eight paintings by Joseph Vernet (p.107).

In 1966 during the curatorship of Halldor Soehner, the Bavarian Hypotheken und Weschsel Bank, whose collection of masterpieces of French and Venetian painting of the eighteenth century is exhibited on permanent loan in the Alte Pinakothek, stepped in, as it were, as patron in place of the Wittelsbach collectors and again brought a new dimension to enrich the Alte Pinakothek. The French section now received works by masters who had previously either not been represented at all or only inadequately: *The birdcage* by Nicolas Lancret (p.101), *The joys of country life* by Jean Baptiste Pater (p.101), the *Pastoral landscape* by François Boucher, the two pastel portraits of the Abbé Nollet and of Mademoiselle Ferrand by Maurice Quentin de la Tour (p.104) and the *Lament of the clock* by Jean Baptiste Greuze (p.106).

The Bavarian Hypothek und Wechsel Bank has continued its activities since 1969 with Erich Steingräber as its adviser. To crown its acquisitions, it purchased in 1971 one of the major works of Jean Marc Nattier, *The Marquise de Baglion as Flora* (p.102), and the famous state portrait of the Marquise de Pompadour by François Boucher (p.105). *Rest by the fountion* (p.103) and another large pastoral landscape painting from François Boucher's early period have been placed at the gallery's disposal as a loan by the Bavarian Landesbank.

ERMINIA AMONG THE SHEPHERDS
Jean Valentin de Boulogne
(b. Coulommiers (Seine et Marne) 1594,
d. Rome 1632), c 1630
Canvas; 135 x 186cm
The theme goes back to Torquato Tasso's
Gerusalemme Liberata (VII, 6-7). In the
painter's late work the *verismo* of Caravaggio
is sublimated in a very original way.
From the Elector's gallery in Munich.
(937)

MIDAS AND BACCHUS
Nicolas Poussin (b. Villiers near Les
Andelys (Normandy) 1594, d. Rome
1665), probably before 1627
Canvas; 98 x 153cm
A scene from Ovid's *Metamorphoses* (XI,
85-145). The connection with Titian's
Bacchanalia is unmistakable.
From the Elector's gallery in Munich. (528)

LAMENTATION
Nicolas Poussin (b. Villiers near Les Andelys (Normandy) 1594, d. Rome 1665), *c* 1626/30
Canvas; 103 x 146cm
A strictly architectonically constructed composition with bold colouring, oriented towards Italian models of the 16th century (Raphael, Titian, Annibale Caracci). From the Elector's gallery in Munich. (625)

CLASSICAL LANDSCAPE
Jean François Millet (b. Antwerp 1642, d. Paris 1679), *c* 1660/70
Canvas; 119 x 179cm
Composed in accordance with the format for the classical Roman campagna devised by Poussin and Claude Lorrain.
From the Düsseldorf gallery. (1018)

THE REPUDIATION OF HAGAR
Claude Lorrain (Claude Gellée: b. Chamagne (Lorraine) 1660, d. Rome 1682), signed and dated 1668
Canvas; 106 x 140cm
At the instigation of Abraham's wife Sarah, Hagar is banished from the house with her son Ismael (Moses 1:21). In this late work, an inner intensity and tranquility have taken the place of the solemn monumentality of Claude's early period. Commissioned by Count Johann Friedrich von Waldstein (along with the companion piece *Ismael in the Desert*, also in the Alte Pinakothek).
From the Zweibrücken gallery. (604)

SEAPORT WITH RISING SUN
Claude Lorrain (Claude Gellée: b. Chamagne (Lorraine) 1600, d. Rome 1682), signed and dated 1674
Canvas; 72 x 96cm
The latest of three versions. The impression is one of solemn order, for which the coincidence of the rectangular lines of the picture's structure with the radial beam of the morning sun, shown almost in the centre of the picture, is essential. Claude is reverting here to compositional methods of his early period.
From the Elector's gallery in Munich. (381

98

▷
THE BIRDCAGE
Nicolas Lancret (b. Paris 1690, d. Pari 1745), *c* **1735**
Canvas; 44 x 48cm
The Arcadian shepherd's paradise, rediscovered by the Renaissance, lives on as a 'staged' pastoral idyll, a veiled dream of paradise, in French rococo painting—especially in the works of Watteau Lancret and Pater.
Formerly in the collection of Frederick the Great in Potsdam. Purchased for the collection of the Bavarian Hypotheken- and Wechsel-Bank in the Alte Pinakothek in 1966. (HUW 4)

◁
THE CONCERT
Nicolas Lancret (b. Paris 1690, d. Pari 1745), *c* **1735**
Canvas; 36.8 x 45.6cm
Probably the oil sketch for one of two versions of a theme termed 'Fêtes galantes' which are recorded in the 18th century but have since been lost.
From the David Weil collection in Paris. Purchased in 1983 with funds from the Friedrich Flick Foundation in honour of Dr Friedrich Flick's hundredth birthday. (14880)

▷
THE JOYS OF COUNTRY LIFE
Jean Baptiste Joseph Pater (b. Valenciennes 1695, d. Paris 1736) *c* **1735**
Canvas; 54 x 66cm
It is not the simple country life of the peasant that is depicted here but the longing of the frivolous urban society of Louis Quinze for the lost paradise. The lovers and ladies dressed according to Watteau fashions point to Pater's great teacher.
Purchased from Baron Alfred de Rothschild's collection in 1966 for that of the Bavarian Hypotheken- and Wechsel-Bank in the Alte Pinakothek. (HUW 7)

CHRIST AT THE HOUSE OF MARTHA
Eustache le Sueur (b. Paris 1617, d. Paris 1655), *c* **1645/50**
Canvas; 162 x 130cm
Christ, accompanied by his disciples, is visiting the sisters Mary and Martha (Luke 10:40). The solemn, classically graceful composition is clearly inspired by Italian High Renaissance models.
Purchased by King Ludwig I from the owner, Cardinal Fesch, in Paris in 1845. (WAF 492)

THE MARQUISE OF BAGLION AS FLORA
Jean Marc Nattier (b. Paris 1685, d. Paris 1766), signed and dated 1746
Canvas; 137 x 106cm
Angélique Louise-Sophie d'Allouville de Louville, Marquise de Baglion (1719-56), was considered to be one of the most beautiful women of her time.
Purchased from New York art dealers in 1971 for the Bavarian Hypotheken- und Wechsel-Bank collection in the Alte Pinakothek. (HUW 19)

WOMAN SCRAPING VEGETABLES
Jean Baptiste Chardin (b. Paris 1699, d. Paris 1779), signed, *c* 1748
Canvas; 46 x 37cm
Chardin's kitchen still lifes enjoyed great popularity — hence the four versions of this composition, the earliest of which is dated 1738 (Washington, National Gallery).
From the Zweibrücken gallery. (1090)

◁

ST BENEDICT REVIVING A DEAD CHILD
Pierre Subleyras (b. Saint-Gilles-du-Gard Languedoc) 1699, d. Rome 1749),
1744
Canvas; 40 x 26cm
Preliminary study for the altar painting, dated 1744, for the Benedictine congregation of the Olivetans in Perugia (now in San Francesca Romana in Rome). Like the Olivetans who were his patrons, the saint and his companions are wearing white cowls instead of the black habits of the Benedictines. The preliminary study *Emperor Theodosius before St Ambrose* for an altar picture for the same Olivetan church (painted at the same time) is also in the Alte Pinakothek.
From the Prince Bishop's residence in Bamberg. (1209)

REST BY THE FOUNTAIN
François Boucher (b. Paris 1703, d. Paris 1770), signed *c* 1730/35
Canvas; 239 x 232cm
Companion piece to *Country Idyll*, also in the Alte Pinakothek, this pastoral landscape uses impressions of Boucher's three-year stay in Italy (1727-30). Probably painted for the Conde de Contamina in Madrid (originally with addition of segmental arch). Purchased in 1976 for the Bavarian Landesbank collection in the Alte Pinakothek. (BGM 3)

MADEMOISELLE FERRAND MEDITATING ON NEWTON

Maurice Quentin de la Tour (b. St Quentin (Aisne) 1704, d. St Quentin 1788), 1752/53

Pastel; 73 x 60

Displayed in the Salon in 1753. The subject, about whom nothing else is known, has a lively presence and is portrayed in a dressing-gown. The works of the physicist Newton were the subject of much discussion in the salons of the time.

Purchased in 1966 for the collection of the Bavarian Hypotheken- and Wechsel-Bank in the Alte Pinakothek. (HUW 6)

THE EARLY BREAKFAST

Jean-Etienne Liotard (b. Geneva 1702, d. Geneva 1789), 1753/56

Pastel on parchment; 61 x 51cm

Painted during his stay in London between 1753 and 1756 and given an English title. The bold infringement of the frame by the maidservant at the left side anticipates artistic methods which were not used until the advent of Japonism in the 19th century (by Degas, among others). Purchased in 1974 for the collection of the Bavarian Hypotheken- and Wechsel-Bank in the Alte Pinakothek. (HUW 30)

▷

PORTRAIT OF THE MARQUISE DE POMPADOUR

François Boucher (b. Paris 1703, d. Paris 1770), signed and dated 1756

Canvas; 201 x 157cm

Jeanne-Antoinette Poisson (1721-1764) became Louis XV's mistress in 1745 and was given the title of Madame de Pompadour. This official portrait depicts not only the beauty of the most influential personality at the court of Versailles but alludes also to her special abilities and intellectual and artistic interests.

Purchased from art dealers in New York in 1971 for the collection of the Bavarian Hypotheken- and Wechsel-Bank in the Alte Pinakothek. (HUW 18)

GIRL RESTING (PORTRAIT OF LOUISE O'MURPHY)

François Boucher (b. Paris 1703, d. Paris 1770), signed and dated 1572

Canvas; 59 x 73cm

The subject, born in Rouen in 1737, served the painter as a model for forty-seven years and became the mistress of King Louis XV in 1753.

From the Zweibrücken gallery. (1166)

THE LAMENT OF THE CLOCK
Jean Baptiste Greuze (b. Tournus 1725, d. Paris 1805), *c* **1775**
Canvas; 79 x 61cm
The clock left behind by the lovers shows
six o'clock in the morning. The title of the
picture could also be 'The Poor Abandoned
Maiden' and could come from a
sentimental, moralizing, social novel of the
time.
Purchased from art dealers in 1966 for the
collection of the Bavarian Hypotheken-
and Wechsel-Bank in the Alte Pinakothek.
(HUW 3)

GIRL WITH DOG
Jean Honoré Fragonard (b. Grasse 1732, d. Paris 1806), *c* **1770**
Canvas; 89 x 70cm
The levity of the subject, signifying the
loose morals of rococo society, is most
beautifully sublimated by the virtuoso,
sketch-like painting. Nevertheless, the picture
obviously had a shocking effect even in its
own time for neither it nor the engraving
made from it was ever allowed to be
exhibited to the general public.
Purchased from a private owner in Paris
in 1977 for the collection of the Bavarian
Hypotheken- and Wechsel-Bank in the
Alte Pinakothek. (HUW 35)

THE DEMOLITION OF HOUSES ON THE PONT
AU CHANGE
Hubert Robert (b. Paris 1733, d. Paris
1808), 1788
Canvas; 80 x 155cm
The bridge of the money-changers was
pulled down in 1788 at the order of King
Louis XVI for reasons of hygiene. Robert
painted a number of such 'journalistic'
pictures, which gripped the public
imagination.
Purchased from a private owner in Paris
in 1968 for the collection of the Bavarian
Hypotheken- and Wechsel-Bank in the Alte
Pinakothek. (HUW 15)

ORIENTAL SEAPORT AT SUNRISE
Joseph Vernet (b. Avignon 1714,
d. Paris 1789), signed, 1755
Copper; 30 x 43cm
Commissioned from the painter, along with
its companion piece *Fishing on the River in
the Evening* (also in the Alte Pinakothek),
by Pierre Charles de Villette in 1751. The
effect of this painting rests essentially — as
it had in the work of Claude Lorrain — on
the significance of the light.
From the Zweibrücken gallery. (2348)

German Painting

The Alte Pinakothek has the most extensive and most distinguished collection of German painting of the late Gothic and Dürer periods. Two series of biblical and secular history paintings with ideal heroes representing virtues, commissioned by Duke Wilhelm IV from the most notable Bavarian, Swabian and Franconian artists from 1528 onwards, were some of the first paintings to be acquired by the House of Wittelsbach. Among these, the *Alexander's battle* by Albrecht Altdorfer (p.123) stands out as a high point of European painting. Wilhelm IV also distributed numerous commissions for portraits. From 1530 onwards Barthel Beham painted a series of Bavarian-Palatine portraits, several panels from which have been preserved. Altdorfer's *Susanna bathing* (p.124) of 1526 may also be numbered amongst Wilhelm's paintings with a high degree of probability on the basis of dating; coat-of-arms and other indications point to its having been one of the authenticated pictures in his possession.

Elector Maximilian I has already been described as the most passionate collector of his generation, and a devotee of the works of Dürer. The acquisition of Dürer's *Lamentation* (p.116) was his first successful transaction, in 1613 the *Paumgartner Altar* was secured for Munich and in 1627 he achieved his greatest triumph in acquiring the *Four Apostles* (p.115), which Dürer had presented to his native town of Nuremberg a hundred years earlier. A study of the inventory begun in 1627 and kept until around 1630 shows that Maximilian had brought together no fewer than eleven works by Dürer. Although his interest in other Early German masters was less keen, he did purchase four Cranach paintings, then the *St John Altar* by Burgkmair (p.116) and a small *Madonna* (now on loan to the German National Museum, Nuremberg) and finally *The Fount of Life* by Holbein the Elder.

During the Baroque period, under the rulers from Elector Ferdinand Maria (reigned 1651-1679) up to Max I (reigned 1799-1825), no substantial additions were made in the sphere of Early German painting, but the secularisation of church property in 1803 brought the appreciable addition of some 240 pictures and this time mainly Early German ones of the fifteenth and sixteenth centuries. Among them were the *Man of Sorrows* by an Ulm master from Swabia in 1457, the wings of the *Kaisheim Altar* by Hans Holbein the Elder, the *University Altar* by a Augsburg master, then the wings of two altars by the Master of the Polling Panels from old Bavaria (p.110), the panels now attributed to the Master of the Tegernsee Tabula Magna from the Monastery of Tegernsee, the Oberaltaich *Man of Sorrows* from the Danube School, the two passion scenes by Wolf Huber and finally Dürer's *Mary as the Mother of Sorrows* from the Monastery of Benediktbeuren. Three other outstanding panels are, from the Abbey church of Aschaffenburg, *Saints Erasmus and Mauritius* by Grünewald (p.118) his *Mocking of Christ* (p.118) from the Carmelite monastery in Munich and Cranach's *Christ on the cross* (p.121) of 1503, also from a monasterial but no longer identifiable source. After Bavaria had temporarily gained control of the Tyrol along with other territories after the Battle of Austerlitz, secularisation took place there also, and notable pictures came to Munich from Neustift near Brixen—the wings of the *St Lawrence Altar* and the *Church Fathers' Altar* by Michael Pacher (p.113), then the *St James and St Stephen Altar* and four scenes from the life of the Virgin by Marx Reichlich.

King Max I's eldest son, Crown Prince Ludwig, was involved with genuine devotion and unquestionable affection in the building up and extending of the collection to a degree that goes beyond any mere amateurishness. The Early German section of the Alte Pinakothek is indebted to Ludwig's collecting zeal, and to the conoisseurship of the very experienced gallery director Georg von Dillis, for Dürer's famous self portrait of 1500 (p.114), his *Portrait of a Young Man* and the likeness of his teacher Wohlgemut (on loan to the German National Museum in Nuremberg), and also for Altdorfer's *Birth of Mary* (p.122), the *St Sebastian Altar* by Hans Holbein the Elder, Burgkmair's *Crucifixion Altar* and his portrait of Schongauer.

In 1827, very soon after his accession to the throne, he purchased out of his privy purse—and in competition with Stuttgart—the 216 Old German and Old Netherlandish panels of the Boisserée collection which had once been admired by Goethe. This meant that Cologne painting, from the Master of St Veronica to Stephan Lochner and the Master of the Life of the Virgin right up to Bartholomaus Bruyn, was represented with a completeness comparable only to that achieved in the Wallraff-Richartz Museum. To these were added the wings of the *Jabach'sche Altar* and the Holzschuher *Lamentation* by Dürer (on loan to the German National Museum, Nuremberg), Altdorfer's forest picture with St George, the Anna Selbdritt portrait by Lucas Cranach the Elder, Stringel's likeness of the Nuremberg merchant Hieronymus Haller and the portrait of the Frankfurt patrician Georg Weiss by Conrad Faber von Kreuznach. In the following year came the purchase of the Oettingen-Wallerstein collection, which had been assembled, like that of the Boisserée brothers, as a result of rather romantic ideas. Two of the pictures thus acquired were the portrait of Oswald Krel by Dürer and Altdorfer's *Danube Landscape* (p.122), the first pure landscape to appear in German painting. In addition to these, other pictures reached Munich from the same source, including Swabian panels, works by Zeitblom and Strigel—among them the full length portraits of Conrad Rehlinger and his children—then, from the Cologne School, the likeness of a master builder by the Master of the Life of the Virgin and the portrait of Hans Leykman (?) by the Master of the St Bartholomew Altar.

Only two years were granted to Hugo von Tschudi as gallery director (1909-1911) but they were years of feverish activity with very fruitful results. In this time he proved himself, as indeed he had done earlier in Berlin, to be one of the most distinguished representatives of his field in Germany. His collaborator Heinz Braune, who was deputy curator of the paintings collection after Tschudi's death until 1914, used his own special expertise to bring together again works from the various external galleries and store-houses. He also discovered Grünewald's *Mocking of Christ* in Munich University and managed to recover this loan, together with the whole of the university gallery, and arranged to have the valuable picture transferred to the Alte Pinakothek.

Friedrich Dornhöffer was a great connoisseur of Old German painting and under his curatorship (1914-1933), the department was supplemented with portraits of fundamental importance, among them *Sibylla von Freyberg* by Strigel, *The Margrave Casimir von Brandenburg* by Kulmbach (p.119), the humanist *Geiler von Kaisersberg* by Cranach the Elder, *Eitel Besserer* by Schaffner and *Christoph Fugger* by Amberger (p.125). In addition to the portraits he added *Mary and the Christ Child* by the Master of the Hausbuch, *St George* by Mair von Landshut and others.

Dornhöffer was followed by his pupil Ernst Buchner (1933-1945), whose scholarly life's work was devoted to researching Old German painting, particularly the Bavarian and Swabian Schools. Among the large number of Old German works that he purchased, special mention should be made of the *Man of Sorrows* by Rueland Frueauf, Baldung's portrait of a Commander of the Strasbourg Order of the Knights of St John, Strigel's *Grave-Watchmen*, works by the Masters of the Aachen Altar, the Erfurt-Regler Altar, the St Bartholomew Altar, the Munich Panels of the Virgin and the portrait of Duke Sigismund of the Tyrol.

German Baroque painting can boast only a few masters of international stature. The three Adam Elsheimer paintings on display, among them the famous *Flight into Egypt* (p.127), came from the Düsseldorf gallery and from the private gallery of Elector Maximilian I. *The Death of Cleopatra* by Johann Liss (p.127) was one of the later arrivals in the gallery, acquired by Kurt Martin in 1964.

▷ △
THE VIRGIN WORSHIPPING THE CHILD
Stephan Lochner (b. Meersburg on the Bodensee (?) c 1400/10, d. Cologne 1451), 1445
Oak; 37.5 x 23.6cm
Reverse side: *Christ on the Cross*. Originally part of a diptych or triptych. Related panels, with the *Presentation of Christ in the Temple* on the inside and *St Francis Receives the Stigmata* on the outside, are in the Gulbenkian collection, Lisbon.
In the Hermann Göring collection, then transferred to the property of the Free State of Bavaria in 1945. (13169)

▷
THE ANNUNCIATION
Master of the Polling Panels (working for the church of the Augustine Canons in Polling near Weilheim, Upper Bavaria, c 1440/50), dated 1444
Pinewood; 129. 5 x 86cm
The upper part of the outside of a wing from a Lady-altar in the church of St Salvator and the Holy Cross founded by the Augustine Canons in Polling. The other wing is in the German National Museum in Nüremberg. The central part of the altar, presumably carved, has been lost. According to the coat of arms, this was the bequest of Duke Albrecht III of Bavaria and his wife Anna, daughter of Duke Erich I of Braunschweig-Grubenhagen. Brought from Polling to Munich in 1803 when the church was secularized. (6247)

ST VERONICA WITH THE SUDARIUM
Master of St Veronica (working in
Cologne in the first quarter of the 15th
century), *c* 1420
Pinewood covered with canvas, gilded
background; 78.1 x 48.2cm
A major work of the late Gothic school of
painters before Stephan Lochner. From St
Severin's, Cologne.
Purchased by King Ludwig I in 1827 with
the Boisserée collection. (11866)

]
BARTHOLOMEW ALTAR
Master of the Bartholomew Altar
(working mainly in Cologne
1475-1510), c 1500/10
Oak; 129 x 161cm (central panel)
Central panel: *Saints Agnes, Bartholomew,
and Cecilia with a Carthusian Donor.* Left
wing: *St John the Evangelist and St Margaret.*
Right wing: *St James the Younger and St
Christina.* A work of the painter's old age
and the last monumental altarpiece of
late Gothic painting in Cologne.
Purchased by King Ludwig I with the
Boisserée collection, the altar having found
its way there from St Columba's church in
Cologne. (11863)

CHURCH FATHERS' ALTAR
Michael Pacher (probably b. Bruneck
1435, d. Salzburg 1498), c 1480
Cedar wood; (total size when open) 382 x
?1cm
Central panel and wings when opened
show the four Church Fathers (Jerome,
Augustine, Gregory and Ambrose) under
painted baldachins. The outsides of the
wings show scenes from the life of St
Augustine. Painted for the church of the
Augustinian Canons Neustift near Brixen.
Brought to Munich in 1812 when the
church's contents were dispersed.
(2597-2600)

THE PRESENTATION OF THE VIRGIN
From a series of pictures representing the
life of the Virgin (altarpiece with wings)
Master of the Life of the Virgin (working
in Cologne c 1460-1490), c 1460/65
Oak, gold ground; 85 x 105cm
The three-year-old Mary climbing the
staircase of fifteen steps after Joachim and
Anna have taken a vow to consecrate their
child to the service of God. Six additional
panels are in the Alte Pinakothek, while an
eighth painting is in the National Gallery
in London.
Purchased by King Ludwig I with the
Boisserée collection. (WAF 620)

THE HOLY FAMILY
Martin Schongauer (b. Colmar (?)
1450, d. Breisach 1491), c 1475/80
Limewood; 26 x 17cm
Mary is handing the child a piece of chicory,
which, according to late medieval flower
symbolism, possessed powers to ward off
evil.
From the Zweibrücken gallery. (1132)

THE PRESENTATION OF THE VIRGIN AND
THE VISITATION
Marx Reichlich (b. near Neustift/Brixe
c **1460, d. Salzburg (?) after 1520),**
signed and dated 1511
Cedar wood; 85.8 x 76cm and 100.5 x
81.2cm
The outside of the left wing of an altar,
carved and painted for the church of
the Augustine Canons Neustift near Brix
Brought to Munich in 1812 when the
foundation was secularized. (2588)

▽◁
THE DEATH OF ST CORBINIAN
Jan Polack (a native of Poland (Cracow
in the Munich area from 1479,
d. Munich 1519), *c* **1483-89**
Pinewood; 147 x 129cm
From the high altar (the lower part of the
inside of the left wing) of the former
Benedictine monastery church in
Weihenstephan near Freising. Other part
of the great polyptych are in the Alte
Pinakothek and in the Diocesan Museum
Freising. The painter's depiction of the
city of Freising and of the Domberg from
south is true to life.
Brought to Munich from Weihenstephan
in 1804 when the monastery's possession
were dispersed. (1402)

SELF PORTRAIT
Albrecht Dürer (b. Nüremberg 1471
d. Nüremberg 1528), signed and dat
1500
Limewood; 67 x 49cm
What is unusual is the full-face, symmetri
representation, which had hitherto been
reserved exclusively for the image of Chr
(Vera icon). The translation of the Latin
inscription runs: 'Here I have painted mys
Albrecht Dürer of Nüremberg, in
imperishable colours, at the age of 28'.
Acquired in Nüremberg in 1805. (537)

Albrecht Dürer (b. Nüremberg 1471, d. Nüremberg 1528), signed and dated 1526

Canvas; 215 x 76cm (each wing)

On two wings are portrayed the monumental robed figures of *(left)* St John the Evangelist and St Peter, and *(right)* St Paul and St Mark. Since Mark does not rank as an apostle, the title recorded since 1538 — *The Four Apostles* — is incorrect. The lower inscriptions, by the hand of the Nüremberg handwriting master Johannes Neudörffer, decry false prophets and sectarians. Bequeathed by Dürer to the Council of his native town. Purchased by Elector Maximilian I in 1627. (545, 540)

PAUMGARTEN ALTAR
Albrecht Dürer (b. Nüremberg 1471, d. Nüremberg 1528), signed, probably 1502/04
Limewood; 155 x 126cm (central panel)
Central panel: *The birth of Christ* (with the Augsburg and Nüremberg patrician family of Paumgartner as the donors, together with their coats-of-arms). Left wing (inside): *St George*, (outside): *Virgin of the Annunciation* (in grisaille). Right wing (inside): *St Eustachius. The Angel of the Annunciation* from the outside has not survived.
Purchased by Duke Maximilian I of Bavaria from the Katharinen church in Nüremberg in 1613. (706)

▽
LAMENTATION
Albrecht Dürer (b. Nüremberg 1471, d. Nüremberg 1528), signed and dated, probably 1500
Pinewood; 151 x 121cm
At the bottom left and right, the donors Albrecht Glim and his first wife Margareth, nee Holzmann (d. 1500), with two sons and a daughter, together with their coats-of-arms. Albrecht Glim was a respected Nüremberg goldsmith. Probably donated to the Prediger church in Nüremberg.
Purchased by Duke Maximilian I of Bavaria from the Imhoff collection between 1598 and 1607. (704)

SEBASTIAN ALTAR

Hans Holbein the Elder (b. Augsburg c 1460/65, d. Basle or Isenheim (?) 1524), 1516

Limewood; 153 x 107cm (central panel)
Central panel: *The Martyrdom of St Sebastian.* Left wing: *St Barbara.* Right wing: *St Elizabeth with three beggars.* On the outsides of the wings in grisaille: *The Annunciation.* One of the earliest Renaissance works in South German painting.
Became state property after being taken from the Jesuit church of St Salvator in Augsburg when the church possessions were dispersed in 1809. (5352, 668, 669)

THE STORY OF ESTHER

Hans Burgkmair (b. Augsburg 1473, d. Augsburg 1531), signed and dated 1528

Pinewood; 103 x 156.3cm
Queen Esther intercedes with her husband King Ahasuerus to save the Jewish nation to which she herself belongs. As a sign of mercy he stretches out the sceptre to the Queen (Book of Esther 2:5,6,7). The impression achieved by Renaissance forms inspired by Venice is one of oriental splendour. The panel belongs to the series of paintings with representations of great deeds from the lives of famous heroes and heroines of ancient times, of the Old Testament and of early Christendom, which was commissioned by Duke Wilhelm IV of Bavaria and his wife Jacobea von Baden for one of the rooms in the Residenz in Munich (cf. Altdorfer, *Battle of Issus*). From the Ducal *Kunstkammer* in Munich. 689)

ST JOHN ALTAR

Hans Burgkmair (b. Augsburg 1473, d. Augsburg 1531), signed and dated 1518

Pinewood; 153.1 x 127.2cm (total dimension)
Central panel: *St John the Evangelist on Patmos.* Left wing (inside): *St Erasmus.* Right wing (inside): *St Martin.* The separated outsides of the wings (Staatsgalerie, Augsburg) show John the Baptist on the left and John the Evangelist on the right.
From the private gallery of Maximilian I. 685)

SAINTS ERASMUS AND MAURITIUS
Matthias Grünewald (b. Würzburg (?)
c 1475/80, d. probably in Halle 1528),
c 1520/24
Limewood; 226 x 176cm
Part of the new furnishing which Cardinal
Albrecht of Brandenburg had commissioned
for his collegiate church in Halle. The

reason for the treatment of this theme v
the cult of Erasmus introduced by the
Cardinal and the revival of the veneratie
of Mauritius in Halle.
Brought from the collegiate church of S
Peter and Alexander in Aschaffenburg
become the property of the Bavarian st
at the beginning of the 19th century. (1(

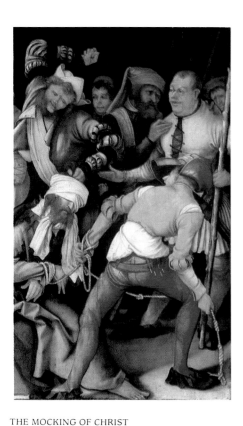

THE MOCKING OF CHRIST
Matthias Grünewald (b. Würzburg (?)
c 1475/80, d. probably in Halle 1528),
early 16th century
Pinewood; 109 x 73.5cm
Christ's head is covered so that he shall
not recognize his tormentors: in the history
of the passion it is written that he should
prophesy who would strike him. The
relief-like structure of the tightly packed
group of figures against a dark background
connects this early work with the South
German art of altar carving.
Brought from the church of the Carmelites
in Munich in 1803/04. (10352)

▷
MARGRAVE CASIMIR VON BRANDENBURG
Hans Suess von Kulmbach (probably
b. Kulmbach *c* 1480, d. Nüremberg
1522), signed and dated 1511
Limewood; 43 x 31.5cm
According to the inscription, this portrait
shows the Margrave (1481-1527) at the
age of thirty-one. The garland of carnations
might indicate that he is a bridegroom.
Purchased from art dealers in Berlin in
1928. (9482)

PHILIP THE WARLIKE, COUNT PALATINE
Hans Baldung called Grien
(b. Schwäbisch-Gmünd 1484/85,
d. Strasbourg 1545), signed and
dated 1517
Limewood; 41.5 x 30.8cm

Count Philip (1503-1548), younger brother of Ottheinrich, Count Palatine, was the son of Ruprecht, Count Palatine of the Rhein and Elisabeth, daughter of Duke Georg the Rich of Bayern-Landshut. From the young Count Palatine's Freiburg period (1516-19), when he was attending lectures on the humanities and law at the university there.
From Neuburg Castle on the Danube. (683)

THE NATIVITY
Hans Baldung called Grien
(b. Schwäbisch-Gmünd 1484/85, d.
Strasbourg 1545), signed and dated
1520
Pinewood; 105.5 x 70.4cm

This Christmas picture is illuminated by three sources of light: from the Christ child as the Light of the World, from the Christmas star (top left) and from the angel seen through the archway, bringing the shepherds the glad tidings. It was probably once part of the decoration of the 'Neue Stift' (new collegiate church) in Halle. Acquired from the collegiate church in Aschaffenburg in 1814. (6280)

CARDINAL ALBRECHT VON BRANDENBURG
BEFORE THE CRUCIFIED CHRIST
**Lucas Cranach the Elder (b. Kronach
1472, d. Weimar 1553),** c 1520/30
Pinewood; 158 x 112cm
The placing of the donor before and to the side of the crucified Christ influenced the standard pattern of the memorial portrait in the period that followed right up to the 17th century.
Acquired from the collegiate church in Aschaffenburg in 1829. (3819)

CHRIST ON THE CROSS
Lucas Cranach the Elder (b. Kronach 1472, d. Weimar 1553), dated 1503
Pinewood; 138 x 99cm
What is striking is the asymmetrical arrangement of the crosses which fit, in a manner previously unknown, into a landscape in which the bitter anguish of the figures is reflected.
Provenance unknown. (1416)

THE BIRTH OF MARY
Albrecht Altdorfer (presumably b. Regensburg *c* 1480, d. Regensburg 1538), *c* 1520
Pinewood; 140.7 x 130cm
Unusual in the transposition of the theme into a contemporary church, which is quite obviously connected with the plans, proceeding at the same time, of the Augsburg architect Hans Hieber for the new pilgrimage church of the 'Schöne Maria' (Beautiful Mary). Found its way from Salzburg (Schloss Leopoldskron?) to become the property of the Bavarian state in 1816. (5358)

▷
THE BATTLE OF ISSUS (ALEXANDER'S BATTLE)
Albrecht Altdorfer (presumably b. Regensburg *c* 1480, d. Regensburg 1538), signed and dated 1529
Limewood; 158.4 x 120.3cm
Alexander the Great conquering the Persian King Darius III at Issus in 333BC. From the basis of cartographical material, the painter came to a completely new, cosmic view of landscape. The panel belongs to the series of paintings with representations of outstanding deeds from the lives of famous heroes and heroines of ancient times, from the Old Testament and from early Christendom, which were commissioned by Duke Wilhelm IV of Bavaria and his wife Jacobea for one of the rooms of the Residenz in Munich. Most of the twenty or so pictures have been kept in Munich, and a few in Stockholm.
From the Ducal *Kunstkammer* in Munich. (688)

DANUBE LANDSCAPE WITH WÖRTH CASTLE NEAR REGENSBURG
Albrecht Altdorfer (presumably b. Regensburg *c* 1480, d. Regensburg 1538), probably shortly after 1520
Parchment on beechwood; 30.5 x 22.2cm
The earliest landscape painting whose topography can be accurately ascertained, which is concerned solely with the reproduction of a particular mood in a forest landscape.
Purchased by King Ludwig I in 1828 with the collection of the Prince of Oettingen-Wallerstein, into which the painting had found its way with the Count Josef von Rechberg collection in 1815. (WAF 30)

ALEXANDER M DARIVM VLT: SVPERAT
CÆSIS IN ACIE PERSAR: PEDIT:C.M.EQVIT
VERO X.M INTERFECTIS. MATRE QVOQVE
CONIVGE,LIBERIS DARII REG: CVM M HAVD
AMPLIVS EQVITIB: FVGA DILAPSI,CAPTIS.

SUSANNA BATHING AND THE STONING OF
THE OLD MAN
**Albrecht Altdorfer (presumably b.
Regensburg** *c* **1480, d. Regensburg
1538), signed and dated 1526**
Limewood; 74.8 x 61.2cm

This rather fairy-tale picture combines two
episodes from the Old Testament story of
Susanna (The Book of Daniel and
apocryphal passages about Daniel).
From the Ducal *Kunstkammer* in Munich.
(698)

CHRISTOPH FUGGER
Christoph Amberger (b. *c* 1500 in
Schwabia, d. Augsburg 1562), dated
1540
Limewood; 97.5 x 80cm
Christoph (1520-1579) was the son of the
Augsburg merchant Raymond Fugger. In
the self-possessed twenty-year-old of this
portrait, we have the embodiment of the
new Renaissance ideal of man.
Acquired from the Fugger estate in 1927.
(9409)

THE VICTORY OF TRUTH
Hans von Aachen (b. Cologne 1552,
d. Prague 1615), signed and dated
1598
Copper; 56 x 47cm
Justice (with the scales) is defending the
naked Truth against Falsehood, stretched
out on the ground. The picture was probably
a gift from Emperor Rudolf II to the
Bavarian Elector Maximilian I.
From the Elector's gallery. (1611)

CHRIST ON THE MOUNT OF OLIVES
Wolf Huber (b. Feldkirch (Vorarlberg)
c 1485, d. Passau 1553), *c* 1530
Limewood; 60.4 x 67.4cm
Part of an altarpiece with side wings
(originally with a semi-circular top edge) in
which was probably depicted the angel,
handing the chalice to Christ. The back
still shows traces of a carved relief. Another
panel with *The Taking of Christ* is also in
the Alte Pinakothek.
From the Prince Bishop's residence in
Passau, when the contents were dispersed.
(8779)

▷

THE FLIGHT INTO EGYPT
Adam Elsheimer (b. Frankfurt 1578, d. Rome 1610), signed and dated 1609
Copper; 31 x 41cm
It has been thought by some that this picture gives an anticipatory hint of the Romantics' capacity for being thrilled by a walk through a soul-stirring night landscape.
From the Düsseldorf Gallery. (216)

◁

DIANA AND ACTAEON
Johann Rottenhammer (b. Munich 1564, d. Augsburg 1625), signed and dated 1602
Copper; 34 x 48cm
After secretly watching Diana and her nymphs bathing, Actaeon is punished by the goddess who turns him into a stag, which is then torn apart by Actaeon's own hounds. A transformation theme, particularly popular with manneristic artists, from Ovid's *Metamorphoses*.
From the Elector's gallery. (1588)

▷

DUCHESS MAGDALENA OF BAVARIA
Peter Candid (Pieter de Witte: b. Bruges *c* 1548, d. Munich 1628), probably 1613
Pinewood; 97.5 x 71.5cm
Magdalena (1587-1628) daughter of Duke Wilhelm V of Bavaria, married Duke Wolfgang von Pfalz-Neuburg in 1613.
From Schleissheim Castle. (2471)

▷ ▷

THE DEATH OF CLEOPATRA
Johann Liss (b. Oldenburger Land *c* 1597, d. Venice 1629/30), *c* 1622/24
Canvas; 97.5 x 85.5cm
The Egyptian Queen Cleopatra committed suicide by means of a poisonous snakebite which, according to Egyptian belief, conferred immortality upon her. Flemish influence, and also that of Caravaggio, are clearly visible in the sensuously flowing style of painting and equally in the buxom fleshiness.
Purchased from Swiss art dealers in 1964. (134 34)

STILL LIFE
Georg Flegel (b. Olmütz, Moravia, 1566, d. Frankfurt 1638), early 17th century
Panel; 22 x 28cm

The rather casual additive arrangement of the objects against a raised horizon points to an early work of the painter.
From the monastery of Raitenhaslach. (5026)

127

Index
Figures in italic indicate illustration pages